TANG OF THE TASMAN SEA

ALSO BY MAGI NAMS

in the *Cry of the Kiwi* trilogy:

Once a Land of Birds

This Dark Sheltering Forest

ABOUT THE AUTHOR

MAGI NAMS studied zoology at the University of Alberta and high arctic plant ecology at Dalhousie University before turning to writing. She is passionate about exploring the natural world and has published dozens of nature articles in the children's magazine *Ranger Rick*. The ten months she and her family lived in New Zealand became the subject of her *Cry of the Kiwi* trilogy. She lives in Nova Scotia, Canada, and is working on her next book, *Red Continent*, about a year of birding, bushwalking, and exploring in Australia. Visit her website at **www.maginams.ca.**

AUTHOR'S NOTE

This is the third book of the *Cry of the Kiwi* trilogy. The first book, *Once a Land of Birds*, chronicles my family's first four months in New Zealand. My husband, Vilis, begins ecological research aimed at helping to rid New Zealand of stoats (public enemy number one of New Zealand birds). My sons, twelve-year-old Dainis [DINE-is], and nine-year-old Jānis [YAWN-is], and I dive into New Zealand history and immerse ourselves in the educational opportunity of a lifetime. We all embrace life in small-town New Zealand, delve into Kiwi culture, and embark on an outdoor adventure odyssey that has us scrambling up volcanoes, hiking over wind-blasted pastures, and trail riding in the shadow of the Southern Alps.

The second book, *This Dark Sheltering Forest*, follows my family's North Island adventures. Torrential downpours and long hours live-trapping stoats introduce my sons to the challenges of doing scientific field research, and all four of us to the lush, cluttered beauty of a New Zealand rainforest. During time off, we hike on the Central Volcanic Plateau, explore a snorkelling hotspot, revel in the blue light of glow-worms, walk among New Zealand's most endangered birds, gaze in awe at towering trees, and stroll among boiling mud pits and steaming lakes in a geothermal wonderland.

This book, *Tang of the Tasman Sea*, recounts my family's adventures during our final five months in New Zealand. The people, places, and events in this book are real. Some individuals' names and identifying characteristics have been changed to protect their privacy.

TANG OF THE TASMAN SEA

Cry of the Kiwi:

A Family's New Zealand Adventure

Book 3: South Island II

MAGI NAMS

For more information, contact Magi Nams at **www.maginams.ca**

Library and Archives Canada Cataloguing in Publication

Nams, Magi, author
    Cry of the kiwi : a family's New Zealand adventure
/ Magi Nams

Includes bibliographical references and index.
Contents: Book 3. South Island II. Tang of the Tasman Sea.
Issued in print and electronic formats.
ISBN 978-0-9937767-2-4 (bk. 3 : paperback).--ISBN 978-0-9937767-5-5
(bk. 3 : html)

    1. Nams, Magi--Travel--New Zealand. 2. New Zealand--Description and travel. 3. Natural history--New Zealand. 4. Ecology--New Zealand. 5. Home schooling. I. Title. II. Title: Tang of the Tasman Sea.

DU413.N34 2015   919.304412   C2015-902223-1
                                               C2015-902224-X

Editing by Pat Thomas
Cover and interior design by Magi Nams
Photography by Vilis and Magi Nams (photo on p. 61 taken by an anonymous tramper on Abel Tasman Coast Track)
Map by Vilis and Magi Nams

Permission to quote brief passages from the following works is gratefully acknowledged:
Laura Sessions – Department of Plant and Microbial Science, University of Canterbury, Christchurch, Interpretive display, on p. 25.
Penguin Books – *A History of New Zealand* by Keith Sinclair, on p. 197.
Department of Conservation visitor pamphlets, on p. 50, 156.

If a permission has been inadvertently overlooked, the author and publisher apologizes and will be happy to make a correction.

FOR THE PEOPLE OF NEW ZEALAND

CONTENTS

OUR TRAVELS
JANUARY– JUNE 2001

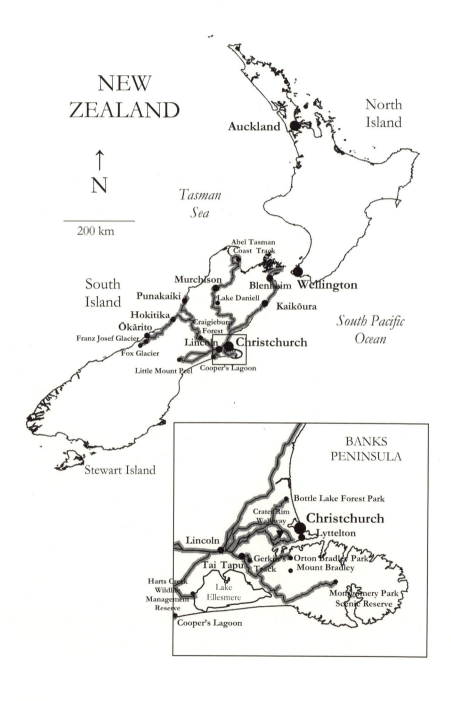

NEW
ZEALAND

North
Island

Auckland

↑
N

*Tasman
Sea*

200 km

South
Island

Murchison

Punakaiki

Hokitika

Ōkārito

Franz Josef Glacier

Fox Glacier

Little Mount Peel

Abel Tasman
Coast Track

Lake Daniell

Craigieburn
Forest

Lincoln

Cooper's Lagoon

Blenheim **Wellington**

Kaikōura

*South Pacific
Ocean*

Christchurch

Stewart Island

BANKS
PENINSULA

Bottle Lake Forest Park

Crater Rim
Walkway

Christchurch

Lyttelton

Lincoln

Tai Tapu

Gerkin's
Track

Orton Bradley Park

Mount Bradley

Harts Creek
Wildlife
Management
Reserve

Lake
Ellesmere

Montgomery Park
Scenic Reserve

Cooper's Lagoon

PREFACE

ALL MY life, I'd dreamed of travelling to far-away countries to hike through landscapes inhabited by exotic animals and plants I'd seen in *National Geographic* or on television. In the year 2000, my dream came true when my husband, two sons, and I left our home in rural Nova Scotia, Canada, and spent ten months in New Zealand.

Our sojourn on the far side of the world was our first extended absence from Canada. As we made our final preparations to travel, we were filled with excitement at the prospect of hiking on volcanoes and exploring tangled rainforests (maybe we'd even see a kiwi bird!) but we also had qualms. Would the tenant renting our house take good care of it? Would our cats remember us when we returned? Would we like New Zealand? Would the kids make friends? Would we be safe?

We didn't pack much to take with us: some clothes, a laptop, binoculars, skates, sleeping bags, and a box of school books. We arrived in New Zealand wide-eyed and unsure of what to expect. Ten months later we returned to Canada inspired and broadened in ways I'd never imagined. Our New Zealand adventure opened our eyes to the world and helped shape who we are.

The *Cry of the Kiwi* trilogy began as observations I scribbled in small notebooks during my family's travels and outdoor adventures in New Zealand, and entries in our homeschooling journal. While living there, I roughed out a few "NZ stories" intended for a private memoir. After our return to Canada, a persistent internal voice told me I should write more of our adventures and turn them into a book.

As happens in life, other responsibilities intruded, with the result that *Cry of the Kiwi* was fourteen years in the making and became one story in three parts: *Once a Land of Birds, This Dark Sheltering Forest,* and *Tang of the Tasman Sea.*

As our New Zealand adventure drew to a close in 2001, I realized that the heart of that country lay as much in its people as in its riveting landscapes and intriguing flora and fauna. Thank you, New Zealand, for the adventure of a lifetime. Perhaps my family's story will inspire others to go adventuring far from home.

Kia ora,
Magi Nams

ACKNOWLEDGEMENTS

WITHOUT THE assistance and encouragement of many people, this book would not be in your hands. Monica Graham offered insightful suggestions for an early draft and instilled in me the belief that my family adventure story could succeed. The diverse and thoughtful comments provided by beta readers Betty Hodgson, Leanne Erickson, Nikki Figueiredo, and Vilis Nams encouraged me and enabled me to polish an advanced draft. Editor Pat Thomas transformed my book dream into a clear and consistent manuscript and discerned that *Cry of the Kiwi* was really three books, not one.

In New Zealand, Christchurch City Libraries staff provided me with helpful contacts and answered numerous questions. Staff at the Māori Language Commission macronized Māori place names for me. Numerous Kiwis offered my family generous hospitality and friendship during our time in their beautiful country – my sincere gratitude to you all! Thanks also to the individuals who allowed me to include their true identities in my story, and special thanks to Andrea and Andy for giving us a home before we found a home.

Last but never least, loving thanks to my husband, Vilis, who supported me throughout this project and rescued me from numerous computer dilemmas. And hugs to my sons, Dainis and Jānis, who didn't balk at allowing me to share their roles in our New Zealand adventure with the world.

PROLOGUE

August 9, 2000

ORANGE STREAKS flare against the night like a beckoning light at the end of the world. I stare through the window at waning darkness while my husband, Vilis, and sons, Dainis and Jānis, sleep onboard the Air New Zealand jet. A strip of cloud below the jet looks like thick smoke, tinged with the colour of ripe muskmelon. Through gaps in the cloud, I see steel-blue waves like beaten metal, and brown peaks like the humps of stampeding bison. A thrill runs through me. *This is it!* These are my first glimpses of Nieuw Zeeland (so named by Dutch geographers for their coastal province of Zeeland). To the Māori, whose ancestors arrived from Polynesia centuries before the Dutch explorer Abel Tasman sailed in search of a southern continent in 1642, this is Aotearoa, "Land of the Long White Cloud."[1]

At 5:00 a.m., a lingering darkness cloaks Auckland International Airport. Groggy from jetlag after flying half way around the world, my family trudges through New Zealand Customs. We're detained by a sniffer dog, a beagle who's detected the scent of fruit emanating from my daypack. If I had any fruit, it would have been a contravention of New Zealand's strict biosecurity regulations intended to prevent pests and diseases from entering the country,[2] however I ate the last dried apricot somewhere over the Pacific Ocean. We're released from the dog's inspection and follow directions that lead us through the airport and beyond its doors. The caress of warm air in the southern winter startles us.

"Look! There's a *palm* tree!" Jānis's voice is filled with

wonder.

Despite our weariness, the sight of those gracefully curved, exotic leaves sparks excitement in us. We're four Canadians 18 000 kilometres away from home (an old farm in Nova Scotia) where palm trees definitely do not grow outdoors!

This is why we came. This is why we left the familiarity of Nova Scotia for the newness of New Zealand. We had a need to explore a part of the world far away, to see new plants and animals and landscapes, to seek new adventures and feel new experiences jolt our senses and expand our horizons. For years, as a homeschooling parent, I'd wanted to live with my husband and kids in a foreign country. Such an adventure would be the ultimate field trip. As the only ecologist on staff at the Nova Scotia Agricultural College, Vilis had for years looked forward to taking a leave to focus exclusively on his research, with no teaching responsibilities. When the New Zealand possibility arose, he and I leapt at the chance. And our sons? Jānis radiated excitement at the prospect of travel adventures. Dainis was torn between the contentment of remaining in Nova Scotia with his beloved home, friends, and LEGO, and the desire for new experiences.

Those new experiences start now, and it's Vilis's research that's made them possible. We've come to New Zealand because of an animal Kiwi conservationists wish didn't exist in their country: the stoat. A stoat is a kind of weasel. It's been declared public enemy number one of New Zealand's native birds,[3] particularly this country's national icon and unofficial symbol, the kiwi. You know the kiwi: dumpy and flightless, almost blind, and with a long beak like a poker. It's the reason New Zealanders are colloquially called "Kiwis." All five kiwi species face extinction, and stoats, which prey on kiwi chicks, are one of the main threats to kiwi survival.[4] This is where

Vilis, who has experience live-trapping and radio-tracking weasels and other predatory mammals in Canada, enters the picture. He'll assume a short-term position with Landcare Research, a government agency that studies and manages terrestrial ecosystems. His research will be aimed at helping to rid New Zealand of stoats.

As we stand in the warm Auckland darkness staring at a palm tree, I feel my family's horizons stretch. What adventures will the next ten-and-a-half months bring? For one of those months, Dainis, Jānis, and I will help Vilis live-trap and radio-track stoats in the Tongariro Forest Conservation Area on North Island, the northernmost half of this country. During the remainder of our sojourn, we'll be based near the Landcare Research branch in Lincoln, a township twenty kilometres southwest of Christchurch in the South Island province of Canterbury. There, as a family, we'll embark on a homeschooling and outdoor adventure odyssey intended to immerse us in New Zealand's history, culture, landscapes, flora, and fauna. As for me personally, I have three goals for my time in New Zealand: lots of hiking, lots of birding, and lots of writing. We've been fortunate to receive the travel and educational opportunity of a lifetime, and I plan to make the most of every minute...

TANG OF THE TASMAN SEA

January 28, 2001

TAWNY RANGELAND at the north end of New Zealand's South Island lies burnt and blackened, fires having swept over the hillsides near Blenheim during my family's six weeks on North Island. We drive south through Marlborough and note that the province's charred rangeland and parched pastures support few or no sheep, a stark contrast to the emerald pastures on serrated hills near Taumarunui in central North Island where woolly white specks trod verdant slopes as far as the eye could see.

We became accustomed to seeing those terraced green hills on our supply runs to Taumarunui, as we became accustomed to the lush rainforest in the Tongariro Forest Conservation Area near Ōwhango where my husband, Vilis, conducted his stoat research, and where I and our sons, Dainis and Jānis, assisted with his research. As a result, the severe drought in north-eastern South Island comes as a shock, though perhaps it shouldn't. Conditions were already dry in the province of Canterbury, south of Marlborough, when we left Lincoln in mid-December to drive to the stoat study site.

Now we push hard south on the coastal highway, pausing to picnic at Point Kean in Kaikōura, a tourist town that advertises ocean adventures such as whale watching, kayaking with seals, and swimming with dolphins. Cold winds blow onshore, and southern fur seals lounge offshore, their brown bodies draped over rocks. During our trip north, we spent a day tramping the Kaikōura Peninsula Walkway and had close encounters with seals and nesting gulls.

Today, we don't linger.

South of Kaikōura, we encounter a road closure due an accident involving a vehicle and train. Fortunately, a gravel secondary road is available to carry us south. The boys bury their noses in books. Dust blows through open windows into "the Blue Bomb," our blue 1985 Ford Sierra station wagon, until we link up with heat-soaked pavement that leads us over eastern Canterbury's rolling hills and agricultural plains to Lincoln.

At our rented house on North Belt, the lawn lies freshly cut by Andrea Byrom, Vilis's associate at Landcare Research. Andrea and her husband, Andy Kliskey, generously hosted our family during our first two weeks in this country. Andrea also helped us find a house to rent, this old clapboard bungalow with a spacious yard, owned by Crop & Food Research.

Two fuchsia shrubs in the front yard dangle rich blossoms. One has pale pink blooms; the other, hot pink. My broccoli plants thrust overripe heads of pale yellow florets into the air. "Close your eyes," Jānis, my nine-year-old, commands mysteriously. I do so, and his small, soft hand leads me to the south end of the house. He instructs me to open my eyes, and I see mounds of cool blue hydrangea blossoms that grace this shaded nook of the yard with unexpected loveliness.

Just as unexpected is the feeling that it's good to be home. Our time on North Island was filled with adventures: driving quads over rough tracks in the rainforest to set and check stoat traps, hiking in Tongariro National Park, and exploring northern North Island through snorkelling and other outdoor adventures. I thought that returning to Lincoln might be a letdown, so it's a pleasant surprise to find that it feels good.

Vilis checks in at his Landcare Research office and brings

home a thick stack of letters and a few small parcels. Our sons dance with excitement, and I nearly do, too! It's as though we've received a second Christmas. While we feast on takeout fish and chips from the local chip shop, cards and letters from Canadian family and friends catapult us into the Northern Hemisphere winter – so much snow! Around us, stale summer heat slowly wafts from the long-locked bungalow.

January 29

THIS MORNING, homeschooling awaits the boys and me. However, first we empty our backpacks and daypacks and store them and our tent and camping gear. I toss dirty clothes into the wash machine and tidy away Christmas mail. Then the boys and I discuss methods of communication and Canadian geography, after which they practice their penmanship.

Vilis and I began homeschooling our sons when each turned five and have continued ever since. We enjoy working with Dainis and Jānis one on one, and treasure the flexibility that allows us to mix and match textbooks from various curriculum suppliers, as well as to plan our own experiments, assignments, and fieldtrips. Our homeschool day begins at 7:30 a.m. with a half-hour of reading aloud to the boys, and ends at noon or shortly after. We don't assign homework, which allows our kids time to pursue their own interests when lessons are done.

As we work, it strikes me that the atmosphere in our kitchen classroom seems artificial and imposed – so different from our days at the stoat research site, where every day was a practical learning experience. My heart tells me that part of me remains in that dark, sheltering forest.

When we finish with schooling, I discover that the small,

weed-infested "before" gardens I cleaned in October are lush with blossoms and vegetables that survived our six-week absence better than I expected. When I planted the seeds and bedding plants beside the bungalow, their rewards seemed distant and uncertain, as did the rewards of this New Zealand trip when Vilis and I planned it back in Canada. But now, I pluck ripe tomatoes from my "after" garden, just as we've plucked sights and sounds and experiences from this country, and see the rewards lying lush and full in my hands.

During the evening, we slam tennis balls back and forth across nets on the courts in Lincoln Domain (recreation park). I miss another volley and exclaim, "Maybe I should take lessons, too!" My twelve-year-old, Dainis, has shown marked improvement in his skills since he joined the Lincoln Tennis Club in October. To the west, the sky is lit with a glorious sunset. Its orange-red rays spill over Lincoln's houses and walled gardens as we re-enter our lives on South Island.

February 2

HEAT WRAPS us in its searing arms and melts us into submission. We dispel our lethargy in the blessed freshness of Lincoln University's outdoor pool and revel in the relative coolness of early morning and evening. During our six weeks on North Island, where frequent thundershowers interrupted summer heat to nourish forests and pastures, we were immersed in landscapes utterly opposed to dry, windswept Canterbury. Now we again live in the Southern Alps' rain shadow. Here, moisture-sucking winds blast across the Canterbury Plain, with its sheared hedges grown to protect pastures from fierce northwesterlies.

At 10:00 p.m., Dainis prowls into my study, where I'm recording our North Island adventures on Vilis's laptop. "Magi, do you know if we have any cylindrical containers?"

"Film canisters," I reply.

"They're too big. We want something…smaller."

"Narrower, you mean?"

"Yes."

"Pen cap." I pull a pen out of a pottery jar on the desk and pull off the cap. "It's got holes in it, though."

"That's okay. We can tape over them." He disappears cheerfully and returns a few minutes later with the pen cap held proudly in his hand. It's packed with a brown substance and sprouts what looks like a wick. "We packed it full of gunpowder and fireworks stuff!" he tells me. (These came from fireworks we bought for Guy Fawkes Day in November.) "We don't know if it's going to be a gun, a bomb, or fireworks. We're going to light it. Would you like to come and see it?"

"That's not the kind of thing a mother wants to hear," Vilis says, mimicking Dainis, " 'We don't know if it's going to be a gun, or a bomb…' "

Dainis sets the gun/bomb/fireworks on the cement sidewalk outside the back door and prepares to light the fuse. Vilis, Jānis, and I run onto the lawn away from the ignition site. Dainis lights the fuse and sprints onto the grass. A sudden blaze of sputtering green, white, and pink flares from the pen cap, accompanied by the pungent smell of burnt gunpowder.

"It's fireworks," Jānis concludes.

Thank God.

Inspired by this experiment, my three pyrotechnicians stride to the rugby field to shoot off some of the remaining fireworks. I let them go without me. Tonight, it seems like a man thing, a thrill-seeking, "southern man" thing.

February 3

VILIS AND I walk briskly, stepping out as though each stride brings us closer to something we can't find in the house, in the yard, perhaps even in Lincoln. The streets are bare grey bellies of emptiness. The trees are hidden behind too many walls in manicured yards.

"I've been aimless all week," I told the boys earlier. "I miss the forest."

"Ah, yes, the forest," Vilis murmured, overhearing our conversation.

Perhaps that's what he and I seek this evening – the North Island rainforest and the remembered sensation of tall trees towering over us – if only in our minds.

"This place sure has a different feel than the North Island, doesn't it?" Vilis says. "Like it's an income level higher, when you look at the houses."

"A level of rigidity higher, too," I add.

"Yeah. As though they're taming the environment."

Of the regions we've so far observed in New Zealand, it's Canterbury that reflects the strict order colonial planners sought to impose in their desire to create a mirror image of England on the far side of the world.

LATER, JĀNIS darts into the study where I'm writing. "Now, we're going to make a paint bomb!"

"Just what a mother wants to hear," Vilis laughs.

"I'll let you know when it's ready, in case you want to watch," Jānis tells me.

"Sure!" I say, in my best supportive-mother voice. "Definitely."

A few minutes later, Dainis shows me a small packet wrapped

with black electrical tape. "It's got gunpowder, four paint balls, and a fuse!"

We all troop out the back door. Dainis places the packet on an upended log and lights the fuse, which spits into life. A puff of smoke belches, then nothing. The paint balls remain stuck within the tape. Five minutes later, Jānis lights the fuse on an adapted version of the paint bomb. This one has a longer fuse that reaches deeper inside the packet. *Poof!* The fuse shoots in one direction, the packet, still intact, in another.

"Wow! The fuse just shot out!" Jānis exclaims.

"It worked kind of like a rocket, didn't it?" Vilis says.

"The gunpowder pushed it out."

"Like a rocket," Vilis says.

"Hey, a rocket!" Jānis crows. "That's a great idea, Vilis!"

"Hint, hint," I murmur.

Later, moonlight and starlight shine through the bedroom window while I lie on the bed listening for explosions. I hear dull thuds and the sharp, gun-like reports of bird scarers in orchards but can't tell if one of the noises resulted from the launch of a nine-year-old boy's latest scientific investigation. 'We're going over to the rugby field to shoot off my rocket, because it might go high,' Jānis told me proudly a few minutes earlier.

My mind is drifting. I can't sort out the noises. With all of a mother's misgivings, I can't sleep either. An arc of awareness curves into the night, one endpoint anchored in my reaching brain, the other skimming the surface of the rugby field preparing for danger, injury, or some other catastrophe. Then footsteps sound on the path beyond the window, and I hear cheerful voices. "It was a flub." Jānis is in my room explaining what happened, but I've already let go the arc.

February 5

IN LATE morning, the coolness of Air Force World in Christchurch welcomes my sons and me, and instantly we know we'll spend hours within the Royal New Zealand Air Force Museum. We view a video of the history of the RNZAF, take in displays of military uniforms, weapons, and medals, and then laughingly try our skill with a Mosquito flight simulator. Mostly, however, we gaze avidly at airplanes, beautifully restored airplanes: Tiger Moth, Vampire, Spitfire, Skyhawk, Avenger, among many more. Some soar beneath the ceilings on suspending wires; some crouch on the museum's floors as though ready for take off. Away from the main display rooms, we tour two restoration hangars where a Sopwith Pup and other planes and parts of planes, including an amphibious aircraft, are in the process of being restored. Dainis and Jānis are enthralled.

An elderly volunteer named Stan guides us through the last part of our museum exploration. He shows us a framed photograph of the Lancaster bomber in which he flew during World War II. The aircraft is massive, dwarfing long lines of soldiers standing on its wings and on the ground below. Our guide tells us he's one of the young men standing atop the aircraft's left wing.

"What was your job?" I ask him.

"I was rear gunner," he replies.

"What was it like, being rear gunner on a plane like that?"

A soft-spoken man, Stan replies, "Cramped." He tells us that he was crammed into a tiny compartment in the rearmost reaches of the bomber, that the flight from England to the German border lasted eight hours and the one to Berlin, eleven hours. For all those hours he couldn't move, had no access to a toilet, and became increasingly cold.

"You must have felt very exposed," I comment.

"Lonely," he replies.

Four hours after entering Air Force World, the boys and I exit its doors and are swallowed by afternoon heat. My sons exclaim again about the yellow Tiger Moth, about the Spitfire and the boat plane. While they chatter, three words revolve in my mind, words spoken by a Kiwi airman who defended freedom on the far side of the world. *Cramped. Cold. Lonely.*

February 6

ON THIS, New Zealand's national day, we catch glimpses of Canterbury colonial history during our visit to Ferrymead Historic Park at the base of the Port Hills in east Christchurch. An Edwardian era museum, the park features collections of antique automobiles and tractors and a reconstructed street scene from the early nineteenth century. A team of Clydesdales clops along a dirt street between buildings with roof peaks that echo the shape of a small volcanic cone on the slope behind them. My sons pat the huge draft horses when the team's driver pulls the Clydes up for a rest.

FERRYMEAD HISTORIC PARK

We stroll along both sides of the street and enjoy period-recipe cookies purchased at the bakery, then laugh at classic silent movies and early cartoons playing continuously in Arcadia Theatre. We look inside a settler's mud house and a cottage, a bookmaker's shop, stable, chapel, one-room school, tailor's shop, and printing shop. At the post office and telephone exchange, my sons and I buy collector's packs of stamps and big brown New Zealand pennies no longer in circulation. The coins' tails depict a *tūī* – a blackish-brown bird with two tufts of white feathers hanging from its throat – perched amid the pea-like blossoms of a *kōwhai* tree, New Zealand's national tree. We also tour displays of antique vehicles and farm equipment. Tractors stand frozen in time, the oldest looking "bare bones" and exposed, with narrow metal wheels. Polished antique cars feature square, conservative cabs and skinny tires that look unprotected beneath airy, arching fenders.

In mid-afternoon, we board an electric tram for a last taste of Ferrymead, the site of New Zealand's first public railway. We've exchanged one learning reality for another. Exit the wild North Island rainforest. Enter the tamer classrooms of textbooks and museums.

February 7

IN THE kitchen, Jānis and Vilis glue tissue paper onto the balsa wood body of Jānis's Spitfire model airplane, which he's been assembling since October. The translucent white tissue forms a mottled skin over exposed balsa bones. With a short-handled bristle brush, Jānis paints the tissue paper with dope, a clear, flammable stiffening agent that permeates the tissue and, upon drying, makes the fuselage sleek and taut. The same compound was used to stiffen and tighten the cloth fuselages of the original Spitfires, rendering them and other early fabric-covered aircraft, potential airborne infernos.

In the living room, Dainis draws bar graphs depicting the percentage of small mammal tracks in the four habitats he sampled within Ōhinetonga Scenic Reserve on North Island as a Scout project. His graph for open forest is as barren as that forest's groundcover. Only one site, of three, produced any tracks at all, for an overall average of 10 percent – all rats. "But look at this!" Dainis enthuses, showing me the graphs for the lagoon-edge habitat. They're the antithesis of the first set of graphs. Tall columns of rat tracks reach 90 or 100 percent at each of the three sites, for an overall average of 96 percent. The riverside scrub graphs show columns of varying heights for both mouse and rat tracks at all three sites, with an overall average of 43 percent for each kind of rodent. The graphs for forest with thick understory show track occurrence as surprisingly stubby bars, considering that two of the sites were adjacent to riverside scrub and all three sites had extensive understories. An average of 33 percent of those tunnels collected rat tracks, while just 6 percent captured mouse tracks. Dainis recorded no stoat tracks in any of his tracking tunnels; nor did I during the four weeks I assisted my husband with his research. This was a good indication of how few stoats inhabited the Tongariro Forest Conservation Area.

"Nice graphs," I comment.

Dainis nods happily. "I like making graphs."

Early this morning, happiness deserted my family when Vilis informed the boys and me that Crop & Food Research has sold this house and property and that we must move out by the end of March. My sons and I groaned and cried out, lamenting the loss of the lemon tree beside the back door, the spacious yard, the torrid pink fuchsia, and the cool blue hydrangeas. Yet now, in the peace of a heat-wrapped evening, that sorrow seems removed, set outside the invisible shield of family bonds.

February 11

SIX MONTHS have passed since we leapt from Northern Hemisphere summer into Southern Hemisphere winter. With a half year of exploration and education behind us, the geographical, physical, and cultural characteristics of New Zealand have settled around us like a comfortable blanket.

This afternoon in summer heat, we head out on our first hike since returning from North Island. It's an easy walk through Harts Creek Wildlife Management Reserve to the western shore of Lake Ellesmere, a broad, shallow lake a dozen kilometres south of Lincoln. Beside Harts Creek, white geese stand out among their grey cohorts camouflaged by rich shadows. Trout flash in the grey-green waters, and cattle graze in creekside pastures edged with thistle and gorse. The gorse is no longer blooming and much of it is burnt and blackened by a farmer's attempt to rid his land of the invasive shrub, which was introduced to New Zealand by English settlers.[5]

A boardwalk provides us with dry footing through willow swamps and leads to a blind. In the lake, three royal spoonbills resemble black-stockinged ladies attired in Sunday-white dresses as they wade and scoop prey from the murky water with broad black bills. I add this species, another "lifer," to my New Zealand bird list. I'm not a twitcher, but birding *is* one of my passions. Pied stilts, mallards, and black swans float far in the distance. The fifth largest lake in New Zealand,[6] Lake Ellesmere stretches toward the horizon like a favourite puddle spilled from the hand of God.

After I scout the birds, we retrace our steps, with the afternoon serene and breezy around us. When we reach the car, we pile in and drive east to Timber Yard Point, where a strong wind splashes waves onto a stony beach. Here, the lake is alive with action of a different sort. Windsurfers glide gracefully over the water. Water skiers toss skiffs of spray. Jet skiers skim over the lake in such a madness of speed it's as though the waves are *flames* licking at their machines.

A few months before my family's departure from Canada, Vilis and I met a young Kiwi man visiting Nova Scotia. When I told him how thrilled we were at the prospect of exploring his homeland, he startled me by saying, 'Ah, New Zealand's boring.'

As I watch the wild jet skiers and recall Queenstown's thrill-o-mania, which we observed in November, I'm more convinced than ever that New Zealanders *invent* danger. Why? Because this country is benign (with the exception of its earthquakes). It has no large, dangerous land carnivores or poisonous snakes, and only one poisonous spider. So, a hike on the wild side doesn't hold the same danger that it might in Canada or Australia. In my opinion, that converts many of this country's residents into danger hunters. Thrill seekers. Adrenaline addicts. And a really cool bunch of people.

February 12

LAST EVENING, Jānis looked at the balsa Spitfire he held in his hands and smiled with satisfaction. 'There! It's finished. Now I can finally take it to Cubs as a Kiwi Project.' He romped out the back door with the Spitfire resting in his hands like a pale bird awaiting freedom.

This afternoon, Jānis again heads out the door with the model in his hands, calling back to me, "I have to figure out how to balance it. One of the wings is a bit crooked." He appears undaunted by the task, perhaps because he pieced together this aircraft bit by balsa bit and its anatomy is known to him, its heart revealed.

Far less has been revealed to Vilis. My husband was unable to complete his planned stoat research project (to determine the distance that juvenile stoats disperse in order to calculate the land

area that must be trapped free of stoats to keep it stoat-free) due to
the small number of stoats in the Tongariro Forest Conservation
Area. So now, he's offered his analytical skills to Landcare's
Vertebrate Pest Management Unit to carry out statistical analyses of
data sets already collected from various possum removal projects.
Australian brushtail possums were introduced to New Zealand in the
mid-1800s for fur farming, but have since become serious pests,
destroying birds' eggs and new-forest growth.[7]

One of the projects Vilis is analyzing is the Tūtaki Valley
Project, his goal to determine how effectively contractors hired to
remove possums did their work. I envision the narrow valley as it was
in September when the boys and I hiked and birded in forests and
grasslands while Vilis helped three Landcare technicians dismantle
two radio telemetry towers. A river rushed cold and strong through
pastures sodden from drenching August and September rains. Mossy,
beech forests dripped lichen and wore the black of honeydew fungus
that I at first thought was charcoal. European goldfinches swirled
across the sky like fairies wearing red-and-white masks, and my sons
and I walked the most peaceful road in New Zealand. *Unforgettable.*

February 13

EXHAUSTED, I stumble into the house after my hour-long Coffee
Club figure skating lesson at the Alpine Ice Sports Centre in
Christchurch, which was followed by my first group tennis lesson in
Lincoln. The latter was a seventy-five-minute parade of instruction
covering handle grip, arm and foot positioning, swing technique and
follow-through, all offered by drawling, weathered Chris Anderson,
who is also Dainis's tennis coach. "Hi, guys," I greet Vilis and the
boys. "How'd schooling go this morning?"

"Well, I read to the boys a lot," Vilis replies gravely, "because we had an accident."

My heart jolts. "An accident?"

"I burned Jānis's airplane."

"*What?*" I see aching shadows of grief in Jānis's eyes.

"I was heating the warped wing to fix it, when it burst into flames. I put the fire out right away, but most of one wing was burnt along with the paper off the fuselage."

Jānis shows me his Spitfire, its balsa frame, a fire-chewed skeleton.

"Can it be repaired?" I ask Vilis.

"Yes, but it will mean a lot more work because new pieces would have to be cut to match the parts of the other wing."

All afternoon, Dainis's and my unspoken sympathy is a gentle blanket comforting Jānis. The boys watch a small blue combine harvest peas in the Crop & Food Research field north of the house, and then gather leftover peas from the ground to use as slingshot ammunition. Slowly, Jānis's grief lifts, and I see a fire of determination replace it.

As planned, Jānis takes his Spitfire to Cubs after supper to present it as a Kiwi Project. Cheerfully, he tells "Akela" Andrew Wallace and the Cubs that he spent five months building the model, that it had more than 140 parts, and that his father burned it this morning while moving a wing. He also tells the Cubs that he's decided to fix it.

February 14

HEAT BUILDS in the house and yard throughout the morning, and it builds in Jānis, too. While a fan whirs in the living room, whipping air into motion, something whirs within my younger son, whipping his temper into motion and causing it to erupt at cursive writing and flare at his other subjects. At morning's end, I tell him, "That's it, Jānis. No movie for you this evening."

"What?" he shouts. "You can't do that!"

"Yes, I can," I say calmly. "Now I suggest you go outside and cool your jets."

Surprisingly, peace reigns for the rest of the day. Jānis putters in the gardens and does his fitness program. Dainis exchanges library books and reads. In mid-afternoon, while Dainis attends his tennis lesson in scorching heat, I drive Jānis to one of his three weekly figure skating lessons in Christchurch. Since he's a competitive skater in Nova Scotia, he's keeping up his training here in New Zealand.

"It's so hot out," I comment to my Thursday Coffee Club coach Chris Street while he sharpens Jānis's skates.

"Thirty-two, I heard," Chris replies.

I wince. "My older son is playing tennis."

Chris nods. "Lobster."

I sit high in the stands, thinking about Dainis frying in the heat and wondering how it is that Vilis and I have two such different children. *What is it that makes them tick?* Here on the ice, Jānis is calm and focused, his passionate energy channelled into jumps and spins. Perhaps for him, the ice is freedom.

On our return home, I exclaim to Dainis, "You're not burnt!"

He laughs. "Chris made us take lots of breaks and drink lots of water."

I smile with relief. "Good for Chris."

Suddenly, I know what Dainis's freedom is – his independence. For almost nine years, since the winter after his third birthday, he clung to me, terrified to let me out of his sight. One day while I dressed his baby brother in winter clothes, he'd walked 200 metres from our house thinking I was ahead of him. When he entered the deep-shaded darkness of a hemlock forest and realized he was alone, he was terrified. When I checked for him outside the house, I heard his screams and ran to him, catching him up in my arms. 'Mama, where *were* you?' he sobbed.

For weeks, he'd cried out in the night. For years, he'd looked around frantically until he located me, calling out in panic if he couldn't see me. Even last spring, at the age of twelve, panic still struck him one morning when Vilis and I walked through the meadow behind our chicken coop, out of sight from the house, causing Dainis to call out in a shaky voice, 'Magi, where are you?'

It's only here in New Zealand that he's discovered the delight of walking alone to the library, tennis courts, stores, and Scout Hall. At last, it seems that childhood terror is fading.

February 16

TAHI. RUA. Toru. Whā. Rima. Ono. Whitu. Waru. Iwa. Tekau. The Māori numbers from one to ten tumble from our lips like jade beads. The boys and I shape the sounds in our mouths, recalling Andrea's instructions for pronouncing the *wh* sound as an *f*, and stretching the *a* in *whā* into the lengthened vowel indicated by the macron above it. This is so little, no more than a glimpse into another culture, one whose forbearers walked the hills of this country when it was still a land of birds. (Until humans set foot on the islands that are now New Zealand, no land mammals existed here except for three bat species.[8])

In early afternoon, Jānis, Dainis, and I sit on the floor in a building in Landsdowne, south of Christchurch. We're one homeschooling family among many listening to storyteller Margaret Copland weave pictures of her English and German-Polish grandmothers' arrivals in New Zealand soon after the colony of Canterbury was founded. We hear of Sarah Stokes's ninety-nine-day voyage on the *Randolph*, one of the first four ships to transport colonists and emigrants from England to Lyttelton in 1850. More than two decades later, Rosalia Gierszewski sailed from West Prussia on the *Friedeburg* and arrived in Canterbury in August, 1872. That ship transported German-Polish emigrants enticed to settle in this faraway land.[9] What did they seek? Land? Adventure? The chance to flourish and prosper? Perhaps all.

February 17

MIST CLOAKS the Port Hills as I run under a sky ribbed with clouds. Goldfinches sing brief snatches of sweet song, and spur-winged plovers cackle like madmen. The paved road beckons, like a long, firm-fleshed arm reaching for me and wearing sleeves of flower gardens and bracelets of hedges. Its perfume is silage, hay, manure, exhaust. Its skin is pebbled and lined. If I had the breath, if I had the legs, I'd let it hold me endlessly, but always I must stop running, and always the road goes on.

In late morning, I pluck a dozen yellow-orange lemons from the back-door tree and squeeze their juice into hummus and guacamole. It never ceases to amaze me that we're living in a country where *lemon trees* grow outdoors! Parsley I grew in my small garden hangs in bunches to dry. Cherry tomatoes gleam like red jewels in a wooden bowl on the white windowsill. It's a small harvest, yet here in my blue kitchen, it's beautiful.

February 18

THIS SATURDAY morning, after Jānis's early skating lesson, we pack food into an insulated bag and pile into the station wagon, heading for Craigieburn Forest, midway up and across South Island. That'll be new territory for us, and Vilis is keen to photograph beech trees and their black fungus and honeydew, a clear sweet liquid produced by sooty beech scale insects that feed on the beeches' sap.

The Canterbury Plain is a patchwork of drying fields and irrigated paddocks. In Porter's Pass, about ninety-five kilometres from Lincoln, the level agricultural land gives way to tawny hills backed by scree-covered grey peaks. Beyond the pass, we reach Craigieburn Forest.

At the forest's edge, a mosaic of tiny beige and orange leaves decorates the ground at the feet of three black-covered mountain beeches. Behind them, the rest of the forest is also blackened by honeydew fungus. Thin, shimmering hairs protrude from the beech trunks, each ending in a drop of clear liquid.

While Vilis looks for photographic subjects, Dainis, Jānis, and I poke around in the forest. The sour smell of fermented honeydew drifts on the air. Sand flies crawl on my bare legs, but seem disinclined to bite. Cave Stream rushes and tumbles, tickling stones in its narrow bed. The boys shoot peas with their slingshots made from forked branches, elastics, and scraps of old fabric.

On a nearby tree, a bellbird clings to the trunk with clawed toes. The sleek, grey-green bird with its yellowish belly is bright against the blackened trunk. Its head bobs while it pecks off honeydew drops. Other bellbirds flutter and clamber about in branches overhead, their liquid notes singing "*forest.*" On hearing their voices, my heart awakens, as though it had been asleep since leaving rich, tangled Tongariro Forest on North Island three weeks ago.

Vilis crouches at the base of a beech tree on which one bumblebee and numerous honeybees rest, oblivious to his camera lens a few centimetres away.

"They're drunk," Jānis sniggers.

Golden against the black trunk, the bees crawl over the fungus-encrusted bark or hover near it, their beating wings blurred.

"Come have a look," Vilis calls. "I've uncovered a couple of the scale insects."

He's scraped away the black fungus, called sooty mould, from several of the multitudinous small bumps that pimple the beech trunk like an incurable case of acne. Within what was one bump (the protective shell or *test* of a female scale insect), I see an orange-brown abdomen with a glistening, thread-like tube projecting from its posterior tip. So, this is *Ultracoelostoma assimile*, the sooty beech scale. The sap-guzzling insect feeds on beech sap by means of a stylet permanently inserted into a sap-bearing phloem cell. Once the insect has removed the nutrients it needs from the sap, it exudes the waste sap as honeydew, which slowly drips from the open end of its anal filament.

Hidden within its protective waxy shell and covered with sooty mould, this scale insect and countless others like it are vital components of the beech forest ecosystem. They provide food for native insects and nectar-feeding birds such as bellbirds, *tūī*, and silvereyes, as well as for the sooty mould that covers the beech trunks.[10]

"Some of the bumps are empty and hollow," Vilis tells the boys and me. "Some have dead insects in them." Once a female scale insect has fulfilled its reproductive drive and filled its waxy shell with eggs, it wastes away.[11]

I'm distracted by a wasp feeding on honeydew. "Wasps are introduced, aren't they?"

"Yeah," Vilis replies. "There's a scientist in Nelson who's doing wasp removal experiments."

I glance around me. "I've only seen one wasp, and I've seen hundreds of honeybees. Wasps don't seem to be a problem here."

Vilis looks up from his camera's viewfinder. "They're not just a problem for the bees. The introduced wasps feed on honeydew, which means there's less for native birds, which means there are fewer birds to pollinate plants like mistletoe."

Since all three of New Zealand's native mistletoe species are endangered, this is a serious consequence. Only bellbirds and *tūī* have learned the trick of twisting off the tips of mistletoe flowers to access the nectar within, at the same time distributing pollen from one flower to another. So here again, an invasive species – the wasp – disrupts a native New Zealand food web and threatens the survival of vulnerable species. In addition, mistletoes' vulnerability is compounded by the actions of other invasive species: brushtail possums feeding on them, and stoats preying on bellbirds.

Farther along the forest track, an interpretive sign relates the Māori legend of the creation of mistletoe:

> MAORI CALLED MISTLETOE PIKIRANGI WHICH TRANSLATES AS "CLIMBING TO THE SKY." WAIPOUNAMU TRADITION TELLS OF TANE, GOD OF THE FORESTS, CREATING FORESTS TO COVER PAPATUANUKU, HIS EARTH MOTHER. PIKIRANGI WAS THE LAST AND SMALLEST PLANT IN HIS BASKET. HE DID NOT WANT HIS SMALLEST CHILD TO LIE ON THE EARTH SO HE PLACED IT ON THE TREETOPS, CLOSE TO THE SKY WHERE IT WOULD BE SAFE.[12]

To me, it seems as though *pikirangi's* safety is as tenuous as the longevity of honeydew drops balanced on their shimmering, silver threads.

In mid-afternoon, satiated with impressions of the beech and honeydew ecosystem and refreshed by our exploration of the forest, we depart for Lincoln. Beyond the car's windows, the steep hills of Porter's Pass are parched, the mountains rising like grey skeletons above them. I gaze at the desiccated landscape and murmur to Vilis, "Earlier this morning I was thinking that since we're getting settled in Lincoln again, maybe it's time to stop all the excursions. Now I think that *no*; there are still places I want to see in New Zealand."

"I definitely want to see more," my husband responds fervently.

The town and the mountains. A church and the sea. The rink and the forest. The courts and the hills. We seem to need them all. The boys have been happier and have shown less sibling rivalry since our return from North Island to Lincoln, where they enjoy separate activities. They've also taken a few steps on the long road to making friends, splashing and riding shoulders at the pool with Scout leader Dave Lord's sons Marcus and Braden. And I've enjoyed returning to skating and experimenting with tennis.

Yet today, my heart leapt with joy at the song of a bellbird. It was as though I'd been hidden away in a prison I hadn't even been aware of, and only with the liquid, ringing notes of that song, realized I was free.

February 20

JĀNIS AND Dainis greet me with mysterious smiles when I plod into the house after my morning of skating and tennis. While I was out, Vilis taught the boys, as he does every Tuesday and Thursday morning so I can have time to myself.

"We're making a surprise for you," Dainis tells me.

"A surprise? What is it?" Over their shoulders, I see thick steam rising like a drifting cloud from a yellow enamel pot on the kitchen stove.

"Soap!" Jānis says. "Take a look."

A blue-grey sludge bubbles vigorously within the old chipped pot, the contents reminiscent of Rotorua's and Wai-O-Tapu's boiling mud pits. The sludge's odour, although not on par with the sulphurous stench of the mud pits, is such that Vilis has opened all the kitchen windows and the door to the backyard.

"What did Jānis use to give it scent?" I ask Vilis, stirring the soap our younger son made using lye extracted from the living room fireplace's ashes. This concoction is his latest Kiwi Project, which he'll present at Cubs tonight.

"Vanilla," Vilis replies. "You should have smelled it before. It smells a lot better now."

I'm too weary and hungry to ask for more details. "My legs are so tired," I groan, then quickly add, "but it's a good kind of tired."

DURING THE afternoon, white butterflies flit about the yard like pale dancers against the greens of hedge and grass. Dainis appears in the hedge's arched opening accompanied by young, red-haired Josh Peters, whose birthday party Dainis attended on the weekend. I wave from the study, and Josh responds with a smile and raised hand.

"*Eee-ew!*" he exclaims on entering the house.

"Messy, eh?" Dainis responds, with some embarrassment.

"Oh, our house gets like that sometimes, too."

They enter the study where I'm writing, all thoughts of housework firmly banished during this short precious time when I have my mind to myself.

"Wicked laptop!" Josh exclaims, seeing the Toshiba I'm using.

"It's my dad's," Dainis explains.

"It's got one of those really good screens. *Supremely* wicked!"

The exclamations continue when Dainis and Jānis show Josh their LEGO Mindstorms Robotics Invention System, their slingshots and pea ammunition, and Jānis's remote-controlled truck, with which Josh is quite taken. It's as though the three of them have to pack as much excitement into this short, unexpected visit as possible. When I take a break from writing to buy groceries, Josh introduces the boys to new computer games. When it's time for him to walk home at 5:00 p.m., he can barely tear himself away from the keyboard.

"Josh, put your other shoe on now," Vilis nudges at 5:15 p.m.

When Dainis's guest is gone, it seems as though a balloon that was expanding and expanding has deflated, leaving a warm gust of new friendship in its wake.

Before supper, I pour off the excess oil from Jānis's cleaning concoction, and he and Vilis empty the dregs of what's left into a small, clear jar.

"You can call it pioneer soap," I suggest.

"Better yet, call it an *experiment* in making pioneer soap," Vilis tells our son.

It occurs to me belatedly that Josh's '*Eee-ew!*' on entering the house was probably a response to the stomach-wrenching reek of the soap!

February 21

THIS MORNING, my kids listen keenly while I begin reading aloud from Elsie Locke's *The Runaway Settlers*. It's the true story of an

Australian mother and her children who ran away from an abusive husband and father and sailed to Lyttelton to become New Zealand pioneers.

"No, don't stop now!" Jānis groans when I close the book after reading two chapters.

I know how he feels. The family is in danger, the mother and two of the children have been severely beaten by the father, and they're still in Sydney. They haven't even got on the ship yet.[13]

"We have other schooling to do, too," I remind Jānis as I hand Dainis a quiz on the endocrine system.. To postpone the academic fireworks as long as possible, I start Jānis off gently with a reading assignment about the human respiratory system. However, by the time his math speed drill is done and his cursive writing practice is in full swing, the schooling explosions have started. Again my younger son rebels at having to do the work I've assigned him, and while his older brother works quietly, he mutters complaints or voices them loudly.

"Jāni, we went through all this last week," I say firmly. "I don't want to go through it again. If you didn't talk back so much, we'd get things done a lot faster and a lot more pleasantly."

He glares at me, but is absolutely silent. *For hours.* Not a word escapes his lips for the rest of the morning.

"You're allowed to talk," I tell him.

'I don't want to,' he scrawls on a piece of scrap paper. He also scrawls answers to questions I ask him or questions he wants to ask me.

"*Mmm.* Good spelling practice," I comment.

He drops his head to the table, smothering a giggle.

It turns out to be the most peaceful schooling morning we've had in ages.

February 22

As Dainis waits at the Lincoln Medical Centre to receive a second treatment for a plantar wart on his left foot, he murmurs for the fourth time, "I hope it doesn't hurt as much as last time." The first treatment was two weeks ago, and afterward, he was ashen-faced, almost fainting.

"Is that Dainis over there?" a man's voice calls out. The doctor to whom it belongs wears short pants and long socks, as did the doctor who administered the first wart treatment. There the similarity ends. This doctor leads us to his examining room with exaggerated strides and a slightly wild look. "So, we're going to kick something in the guts again today, are we?" he asks.

Disconcerted, I respond, "Dainis is here for a second wart treatment."

"Exactly. When you've kicked someone in the guts and he's rolling around holding himself and hollering, '*Ow, ow!*' and you kick him in the guts a second time, it's a lot harder for him to get up again, isn't it?"

Uncertain, Dainis, Jānis, and I nod.

The physician questions us about the history of Dainis's wart, examines it, and brings forth the thermos of liquid nitrogen.

"The last time, it hurt a lot," Dainis says nervously.

"We-e-e-l-l, what we have to do is cool it off. Cool the wart off before we kick it in the guts." The doctor waves a long cotton swab like a magician's wand, pokes it into the nitrogen, then sweeps it back and forth in front of us, swirling white mist through the air. He dips the swab into the nitrogen again and rubs it in quick circles over the ball of Dainis's foot. "Does that feel cool?"

Dainis nods.

"Then, when it's all cool…" Again, the swab is dipped in the steaming liquid nitrogen. Again swirled briefly through the air. Now pressed against the wart for a few seconds, then released. "...we kick it in the guts again and yell, '*I hate you, wart. Get away from me!*' "

The boys stare open-mouthed. I fear they think he's a madman. And yet he's gentle.

"It's true," the doctor tells us. "Studies have shown there is a strong psychological link between the mind and the body. So, every day, I want *you*," he nods at Dainis, "to talk to your wart; to tell it that you hate its guts and want it out of you. Got that? And not in a nice way. You'll have to yell at it."

Dainis looks as though he's not quite sure about all this, but he nods, as though to humour the doctor.

The medical magician dips the swab into the nitrogen again, then sprinkles liquid onto his bare thigh. It evaporates instantly. "Do you know how cold liquid nitrogen is?" he asks.

We shake our heads.

"Do you know the temperature at which water boils?"

We nod.

Jānis flinches when the wet cotton swab moves toward his hands, a trail of white mist following it.

"Liquid nitrogen is twice the temperature of boiling water, but in the opposite direction."

I remain motionless, curious, as the swab shakes clear, liquid drops onto my bare knees. I feel only the briefest sensation of coolness before the drops disappear into the air. "It just feels cool," I tell Jānis.

More drops are sprinkled in fun. Onto Dainis's foot. Onto Jānis's hands. The boys smile.

"I think this bloke," another nod to Dainis, "deserves a chocolate paddle pop. There aren't many who would be as brave as he was."

"I'm not sure," I say, finding it hard not to smile. "We were just at the dentist's this morning."

"What is a chocolate paddle pop anyway?" Jānis asks.

"Oh, it's a frozen flat chocolate thing. Or sometimes you can get it in a little cup with a spoon. A chocolate paddle pop doesn't have much sugar in it, and it has lots of milk in it, so it's really very good for teeth."

"I've seen them at the dairy," Dainis pipes up.

"What about me?" Jānis asks. "I had more done at the dentist than he did."

"Maybe you could have it for pudding (dessert)." The doctor turns his rather wild gaze on Jānis. "And *you're* going to help your brother remember to yell at that wart of his. Every day. Right?"

Janis nods.

We leave the office, with Dainis cheerful and Jānis grinning.

What can I do?

I buy the chocolate paddle pops.

DARKNESS HAS already fallen when I stroll the two-minute walk to the Lincoln Scout Hall to bring the boys home after Dainis's Scout meeting. (Jānis went over earlier to meet Dainis, but neither son has returned home.) The balmy night captivates me, and a longing sweeps through me. I could hold this warm evening air forever and gaze at stars sprinkled across the sky until they are no more.

I hear my sons' voices and see them lounging outside the Scout Hall with Marcus and Braden Lord, the Scout leader's sons. The four boys are half-caught in darkness, half-illuminated in the orange glow of street lights that accentuate Dainis's tan Scout uniform. The other two Scouts' dark green uniforms appear as deep blurs of shade topped by pale faces that shift in size and shape with movement. I feel like an intruder.

"Hi," Dainis calls out, spotting me. "What are you doing here?"

Somewhat taken aback, I tell him gently, "It's time to come home."

Even as I speak, the Scout Hall door opens, spilling startling white light onto the scene. Scout leader Dave Lord strides to his car, one arm full of papers, a briefcase in the other. He pauses when he sees me. "Sorry. It took a long time to prepare all the camping gear. You must have been getting worried."

I shrug, thinking more in terms of Jānis's regular bedtime, now long past. "I just thought it was time for them to come home."

"Bye, Marcus! Bye, Braden!" my sons call. Dainis grins. Jānis is almost skipping.

"What did you do after Scouts?" I ask the boys. I know that during the meeting, the Scouts made preparations for a weekend camp at Blue Skies Conference and Training Centre in Kaiapoi, a few kilometres north of Christchurch. Blue Skies is owned by the national Scouting organization, and several Scout Troops have jointly booked the facility, which offers abseiling, obstacle courses, and other challenging outdoor activities.

"We played soccer, then helped get the cooking stuff ready," Dainis replies.

"That was fun!" Jānis adds, his feet dancing, his hair gleaming like strands of tossed silver beneath a street light.

February 23

DARKNESS CARESSES me when I set six empty milk bottles on the grass near the curb, a red plastic token for each jingles in one of the bottles. Sometime in early morning, the milk man will replace the empty bottles with full ones.

Wind pushes aside tree leaves with a delving, restless hand. Above me, the sky is a torn patchwork of cloud and stars. I feel the wind's restlessness echoed in me. All day I fought to write, snapping at the boys when they interrupted me and impatiently answering their questions about schooling assignments. My annoyance was further fuelled when the groundskeeper for Crop & Food Research dropped by the house to request that the boys not wander in the harvested pea field because of the extreme fire risk. Then my annoyance spread to Vilis, since it was he who had told the boys to explore that field. Yet, with one comment from Dainis, at whom I'd earlier lashed out, all my annoyance and frustration wilted. Jānis asked to use the laptop for a few minutes, and Dainis shouted from the living room, "No! She has to WRITE!"

It sounded like a dirty word.

My typing became gentler, and I spent the afternoon regaining my hurt and suspicious sons' trust. After tea, I made peace with Vilis. Now, in late evening, I drink in the restless wind and sky, then return to the house where the laptop awaits my efforts to record our adventures in this land.

I know this is a season in my life, a season filled with the demands of educating my sons and being Mom's Taxi, a season when commitments to my children outweigh the time I allot to my own interests. I also know this season will pass, although that didn't ease today's frustrations. Eventually, I'll get my brain back. Even now, I can truly say that the one priceless gift homeschooling has given me is that I've come to know my sons well.

February 24

IT'S BEEN five months to the day since a September thunderstorm whipped rain down onto Gerkin's Track in the hills near Tai Tapu (a village near the base of Lyttelton Volcano southeast of Christchurch) and thwarted my family's hiking plan. From the shelter of the station wagon, we watched a tom turkey display his magnificent tail feathers and knew we'd return.

This afternoon, dried pastures surrounding Gerkin's Track roll like silver seas in the sun's glare. Weary from his early morning skate, Jānis grumbles while he climbs over a wooden gate. He tumbles onto a bed of springy, dried grasses and fakes a snooze. Vilis and I cajole him into continuing on the track. (Dainis is at the Scout camp at Blue Skies.) The track leads us over rolling hills the colour of a lion's coat, where we're rewarded with sightings of rabbits, feral goats (one a magnificent brown-and-white billy with wide, flaring horns) and a small, decrepit hut beside the dirt track. The hut's beige mud walls are almost hidden by gorse.

Jānis perks up. "What's that?"

"It looks like a mud hut," I say.

"Like the mud house we saw at Ferrymead!"

Warily, we circle the hut to avoid the prickly gorse until we find a gap that allows us approach the structure. Weathered trunks of slender, long-dead trees at the hut's corners support thick mud walls. An uneven smile of cracked grey boards creates a gable capped by rusted corrugated metal sheeting.

"Do you think it was built by settlers?" Jānis asks excitedly.

"The original structure might have been," I reply, "but the roof is definitely more recent."

Vilis peers around the boards into the hut's interior. "The farmer who owns this land must use it as a storage shed now. There are cans of something in it."

We leave the hut and tramp on through a pasture tufted with neat rows of pine saplings – the farmer's retirement income, when the trees mature. Far ahead to the north, Gibraltar Rock raises its clean volcanic profile to the sky. Beyond it, the barren rocky lumps of Cooper's Knob on Lyttelton Volcano's crater rim bulge upward like tumours on the brow of the earth.

JĀNIS ON GERKIN'S TRACK, WITH GIBRALTAR ROCK (LEFT) AND COOPER'S KNOB (RIGHT) IN THE BACKGROUND

As we hike, heat pours down. Sheep seek shade beneath overhanging pine boughs at pasture edges. Sweat drips off us, and we gratefully sink down into the narrow shade offered by a tall gorse clump. While we rest, we're lulled into lassitude by white, cotton-candy clouds on a royal-blue sky and the lazy buzzing of insects. To the south, distant haze blurs the Canterbury Plain's tall hedges and veils Lake Ellesmere, truly Te Waihora, "The Spreading Water," as the Māori call it.

"A harrier!" Jānis points to the sky, and we watch the long-winged hawk soar on thermals and turn in circles until out of sight.

"Hey, the gorse is starting to bloom again!" Jānis indicates yellow flower buds among the shrub's spikes.

Like a wake-up call, the sight of those buds instantly drives home the fact that we only have four more months in New Zealand. Last August when we arrived in Canterbury, gorse was in full bloom. Soon it will bloom again, as autumn arrives, and then winter and our departure from this country.

That departure suddenly seems much too close. Since our return to Lincoln from North Island a month ago, life has felt anticlimactic. We've slipped into adventure inertia and have taken only three short, easy walks that don't even merit being called "hikes." Yet, our exploration wish list still includes West Coast rainforests and glaciers, as well as backpacking the Abel Tasman Coast Track, one of this country's Great Walks. Each of those excursions will require driving across the Southern Alps. As winter approaches, weather will deteriorate, affecting travel, as well as camping and tramping opportunities.

"Time to go," Vilis decides.

We rise to battle the sun, just as my family must battle this adventure inertia to make our wish list our reality.

February 25

THE TRUNKS of pine trees, painted green by fungus, flash past Vilis, Jānis, and me like neon signs. Fine, loose sand sucks at our sneakers as we run a 4.8-kilometre orienteering course we've chosen as beginners. This is a race, using a map and compass, to find seventeen orange and white *controls* (markers) set in Bottle Lake Forest Park north of Christchurch.

Roots and stumps create low barriers over which we leap, and our breaths rasp in our tired throats. Fantails call out "*kip!*" at our passage, as though encouraging us to hurry. At control after orange-and-white control, Jānis punches our card with the unique pattern for each location. Then we consult the map and run for the next control.

Trails criss-cross the park, providing many choices for routes to follow. Jānis and Vilis reach out to pluck ripe blackberries as we race through a cut-over area. We enter the forest again and make a dash for the last five controls, which are mercifully spaced closer together than the previous dozen. Jānis punches our card at control #619, and we sprint through bracken and trimmed branches to the finish line. Our time is 58 minutes, 10 seconds, which places us in the top ten family groups.

"That was fun," Vilis pants, his face red, his chest heaving.

Jānis and I agree. Clouds spit drizzle onto our sweating bodies as we all sip diluted Powerade.

IN LATE afternoon, I hear voices in the yard and see Dainis trudging home from the Scout Hall after the Lincoln Scouts' weekend camp at Blue Skies. The duffle bag containing our tent swings heavily in his hands. Two other Scouts, Braden and Marcus Lord, accompany him.

I greet the three boys outside. "Hi! How was Scout Camp?"

"Good, but we were the only troop there," Dainis says dully.

"Yeah. All the other troops pulled out," Marcus grumbles. "If we'd known, we would have pulled out, too."

"Didn't you enjoy it?" I ask.

"Yes, but it's just that it was like a troop camp," Braden explains, "and we couldn't do some of the things we were going to do, like abseiling, because the other troops didn't come."

Dainis's face is pale with exhaustion, his T-shirt and jeans smudged with dirt. "We didn't even need *this*." He drops the tent at my feet.

Marcus and Braden stay only briefly, but I hear Dainis and Jānis arranging a visit at our house after school on Friday. After the other Scouts leave, Dainis flops into a chair beside me in the study and grimaces. "My arms and the insides of my elbows are sore."

"From what?" I ask.

"We had an obstacle course. It was really fun, but we had to swing on a rope to a net, then climb up one side of the net and down the other. We did it a bunch of times."

"That would do it." I study my weary son and ask, "So, even though the other troops pulled out, are you glad you went?"

He grins hugely. "Oh, *yeah*."

February 27

MY MIND swirls with edges: right outside, left inside, right inside, left outside, right inside, left inside. They all slither together into what Chris Street calls "a nasty dance to teach" – the Baby Blues. I clutch at his guiding words, struggle to make my skates do the correct movements, and finally, miraculously, feel it click.

Then Kim Lewis hustles me and nine other Coffee Club skaters into precision elements in preparation for the fall gala to be held in early April. Within seconds, I'm pumping backward like I never have before – arms extended, hands holding onto those of two other skaters. We circle an imaginary spot on the ice, our collective momentum carrying us into heady speed. Then we glide to a stop and laugh. Along with my skating friend, Sabrina, and several other skaters, I expel a tense breath of relief. It's a heady feeling to know I'm capable of much more than I'd believe.

THROUGHOUT CANTERBURY, the hot, dry weather continues, with

the wind blasting out of the northeast. Our lawn is brown, tough, and crisp. The soil in my garden is hard grey dust. A front-page headline in Christchurch's *The Press* reads: EXTREME CARE URGED AS REGIONAL FIRE RISK SOARS. When I visit the butcher shop to buy lamb chops and mince (ground beef), I ask when the heat will end.

"Oh, after the middle of March, the weather starts changing," the man at the counter assures me. "You have your shorter days then. Now, everybody's cleaning up their gardens, getting ready for the change. Getting ready for winter."

"So, it'll be cooler and rainier then?"

He nods. "But you'll still have some nice, warm days. Even in winter, you'll have some sunny days. On mornings when there's a good, thick frost, the afternoons warm up real nice. Lots of people like to have the frost, because then they know they'll have a sunny, warm afternoon."

His statements remind me of our first frosty night at the old bungalow in late August. *We were so cold!*

"Do you get snow here?" I ask.

He shakes his head. "Nah. Not very often. My kids still get excited when it snows."

"Do you get freezing rain?"

He tilts his head. "Hail, you mean? We get some good hail storms, usually at the end of winter."

"No. I mean the rain freezing as it falls. It coats everything in ice. In Nova Scotia, it's a real problem. It can bring down power lines."

He shakes his head. "Black frost. We have that. That's when it rains, then the ground freezes overnight and you can't even tell there's ice."

I nod. "We call that black ice."

Another customer enters the shop, so I gather my meat and leave, glad that my family has decided to backpack the Abel Tasman Coast Track next week before the time changes and early evenings bring early darkness.

February 28

A BLACKBIRD chatters, luring me into the dawn. Not a breath of wind stirs birch leaves' jagged hearts, and cabbage trees' spiky leaves are daggers poised against the morning sky. Mist rises from fields and drapes the feet of the Port Hills, thickening into fog along Birches Road. Cars' red eyes disappear into its whiteness, and I feel like I'm walking into oblivion.

AFTERNOON SUN pierces a clear blue sky as I harvest string beans and press a sun-warmed tomato against Dainis's cheek before filling a large bowl with the red fruit. I pull out old lettuces grown into tiers of leaves and the broccoli plants Dainis beheaded on our return from North Island, which have since produced only spindly florets. I leave the tangled forest of tomato vines and the tidy plantations of parsley, onions, and sweet basil. To my left, hollyhocks I planted in October still ruffle deep rose petticoats in the afternoon breeze. To my right, the shrub fuchsia I pruned in September dangles hot pink pendants. Back home in Canada, my gardens and flowerbeds lie asleep beneath a blanket of winter snow. *What condition will they be in when we return?*

Jānis stands barefoot beside me and looks sadly at the yard. "When we leave, whoever has bought this land will probably just tear up the garden and hedges."

"They might," I say. Nonetheless, I'll take with me what's mine: the gentle-faced pansies, fiery orange impatiens, icy blue lobelia, other flowers, parsley, and chives I planted. They'll provide a tendril of continuity in our move from one home to another.

Jānis's sad comment stays with me while I garden. An unexpected reward of my family's time in New Zealand has been the insights we've gained into each other's psyches through the challenges we've faced: loneliness, homeschooling tensions, disagreements, demanding physical adventures, sibling rivalry, and now the impending move to a house we haven't yet found.

Later, as we drive home after an evening dip in the Lincoln University pool, Jānis, who has let go of his sadness, summarizes some of his observations about New Zealand. "Every small town in New Zealand has a dairy, a take-away fish and chips and burger place, a rugby field, and—"

"A tennis court," Dainis interjects.

"Yes, a tennis court. And a pub. And every small Canadian town has a rink."

So. This is the character of two nations as summarized by a nine-year-old observer.

March 1

TWO HEDGEHOGS appear as small dark shadows against blue evening light. They race across the driveway when I pass through the hedge's arch. Now I know what's been rooting in my gardens and tossing grass-clipping mulch onto cement paths.

The evening breeze is sweet and warm, a loving caress out of the northeast. Above me, violet clouds of carded wool blanket the sky. In the west, a band of brilliant blue speaks of some other world beyond the clouds. The Scouts are late returning from practicing for their Athlete Badge, but it's no hardship to rest against a car in the warm dusk and chat with other mothers about the weather, about the night, about travelling to distant parts of the world.

A tall figure and small figure join me, both smiling, and I'm happy – and relieved – to see that my husband and younger son's relationship survived this morning's schooling crisis, when Jānis's unrelenting rage at long division tore Vilis's heart. I had intervened and reprimanded Jānis, but Vilis was too upset to continue the lesson. He inline skated to Landcare. Jānis flung himself onto his bed, and Dainis entered the kitchen looking as though he'd been caught in a crossfire.

The afternoon passed quietly, as though in waiting for a resolution to the morning's difficulties. 'Ask Vilis to help you fix your plane after supper,' I suggested to Jānis, knowing that he and Vilis needed to work through the long division fiasco to find the light on the other side. It's even possible that Jānis's math outburst was a delayed response to his Spitfire model being accidentally burned by Vilis.

After tea, Jānis was all contrition while he and Vilis worked together to replace the tissue paper on the damaged Spitfire. Slowly, the conversation of these two, who are so much alike in so many ways, eased away from overly bright chattering on one side and long periods of silence on the other until I caught phrases indicating a discussion of this morning's schooling debacle.

And now, they're smiling. The Scouts straggle back from the high school. After the troop is dismissed, my family strolls home in the warm night air, incredibly drained, incredibly tired, yet one. Always one.

March 2

I SCRUB at study, kitchen, and living room windows and am rewarded by clear panes, like eyes into the soul. Dainis and Jānis scurry around, checking off items on today's housecleaning list as they're completed, excited because their new friends Braden and Marcus Lord are coming over after school.

Suddenly, Braden is here, and the excitement level rises. The boys show him their slingshots and make one for him.

"I see you're cleaning lots of windows," Braden comments to me politely.

"Yes, I've been at it all day," I reply.

"If you were working, how did Jānis and Dainis do their school work?" he asks.

I laugh. "Oh, they had their assignments this morning, and I supervised them in between doing windows. If they had questions, they just came and asked me." Today, schooling slid by smoothly as though some new pane into learning had been opened, inviting in fresh air.

Braden turns to Dainis and Jānis. "With homeschooling, it must be harder to make friends."

Jānis swings his foot back and forth.

Dainis shrugs. "Yeah."

Then they're off, exploring and shooting slingshots. When Marcus arrives, he's instantly caught up in their excitement. The house and yard nearly dancé with ricocheting energy, to say nothing of peas blasted from slingshots.

March 3

AGAIN, THE house is alive with young lads holding slingshots or improvised swords. Dainis, Marcus, Braden, and Jānis come to Vilis or me for repairs or sticky plasters (bandages), and I hear boy jokes and excited laughter and snickering. Growing-boy appetites devour lunch, after which the kids race about in the yard.

IN LATE afternoon, Jānis crams clothes, snorkel and mask, rain gear, a towel and facecloth, and some food packets into Vilis's big daypack, which will be his to carry on our extended tramp of Abel Tasman Coast Track. One of New Zealand's Great Walks, this fifty-one-kilometre track follows the coast along the top of western South Island. Its southern trailhead is at Marahau, and its northern gateway, at Wainui.

Although Dainis backpacked with the Lincoln Scout Troop on Mount Somers in November, the Abel Tasman Coast Track will be our first backpacking adventure here in New Zealand as a family. Since we'll be on the track for five days, we must carry all our food, clothes, shelter, first aid supplies, and other necessities.

We've carefully planned lightweight meals and bought a small, light tent for the boys to sleep in. Vilis has spent hours sewing a lightweight fabric shelter for his and my nights, and he and I have carefully chosen which cooking implements to bring on the trek. It's all about weight. Now, Vilis weighs Jānis on a borrowed scale, then weighs him with the full daypack on to ensure that it weighs no more than a quarter of his weight. This is the standard the Scouts use.

"Okay." Vilis gives Jānis the nod and begins the same weighing procedure with his own, Dainis's, and my backpacks. Excitement and anticipation fill the house, as they did in Ōwhango before we tackled the eight-hour Tongariro Alpine Crossing in mid-January. Abel Tasman Coast Track will present us with a different set of challenges – the two biggest are having the strength to carry a backpack for days in a row, and having the endurance to finish the trek. We'll see how we fare.

"Is it all right if I trim the hedge now?" Jānis asks.

"Sure," Vilis tells him.

Jānis collects the old, rusted pruning shears we bought at a recycling depot months ago and marches cheerfully out the door, saying firmly, "We can't move away from this house with the hedge looking like *that*."

"*That*" is pruned to a straight, level surface by the neighbours on their side of the hedge but sprouting leggy shoots of uneven heights on our side. Like a really bad haircut, it assaults the eyes. Jānis, who may blow up while working through a math problem or laugh uncaringly when told an excavator will be needed to clean his half of the boys' bedroom, hums serenely. His face is filled with contentment as he slices stem after unruly stem from the thirty-five-metre hedge.

March 4

EARLY ON this Sunday morning, we climb into the Blue Bomb and begin our journey to Marahau, the southern trailhead of the Abel Tasman Coast Track, 450 kilometres northwest of Lincoln. In the west, the Southern Alps are whispers of grey hidden by mist. Spur-winged plovers stand like sentinels in mowed fields. Christchurch streets roll out like empty grey tongues in yawning mouths, and the city's walled gardens have been beaten into submission by the heat, their lawns brown and dry. On national radio, we hear that the last rats were removed from Kapiti Island in 1996 and that the island, which is now free of all introduced predators, supports flourishing populations of robins, saddlebacks, *weka* (woodhens), and red-crowned parakeets.

At Amberley, north of Christchurch, clusters of brightly clad cyclists hunch over their wheels. Farther north, Lombardi poplars stand slim and elegant against a backdrop of hills the colour of a lion's coat – the Puketeraki Range. Magpies fly up from fence posts along the highway like black-and-white pirates bent on pillaging the already parched pastures where grey-woolled sheep stand half-hidden in a sea of bleached grasses.

At Waipara, we drive into the hills, their slopes as brown as the clay-sand soil exposed by road cuts. Willows' yellowed leaves droop in late summer heat, and rivers lie shrivelled in their broad stone beds. Like a band of travellers in a harsh land, sheep plod single file across a steep slope, the wool on their backs spun into gold by the sun's slanted rays.

North of Hurunui, clouds puff streams of white cotton onto the lower slopes of grey-brown peaks – the Hanmer Range to the north and the Lowry Peaks Range to the east. Here, the highway is edged with long, lush, irrigated paddocks – a green and expensive contrast to the surrounding arid landscape. Yet, gone from the paddocks both here and elsewhere are the *pūkeko*, mallards, and paradise shelducks we observed in mid-September when we drove this same route to Murchison and then to the Tūtaki Valley possum study site.

We turn west and parallel the Waiau River. To the north, the river's eroded banks plunge from high plateaus. To the south, its flanks are grazed by meaty steers. Farther west, native scrub and pine plantations patch sun-scorched slopes. Scotch broom, bracken, and *mānuka* edge the highway. This is rugged country comprised of valley paddocks, jutting hills, and an isolated road with nothing beyond Culverden except a highways depot and sheep station signs: GLYN WYE STATION, GLENHOPE STATION.

On the approach to Lewis Pass, Vilis exclaims, "Look! There's a stoat! Running across the road!"

Slender body stretched to the limit, scrawny tail flopping behind, the small weasel races across the pavement into a rocky clearing.

"You're not a true New Zealander," Dainis chides Vilis.

"Yeah. You should have driven right in there after it," Jānis teases.

Vilis glances at the rocks. "Into *that*?"

At Springs Junction, we turn north, and Dainis begins our road trip rhyming-word game by saying demurely, "This is a lovely New Zealand beech forest we're driving through."

"Therefore, I'll have a poo!" Jānis laughs.

"Uh-oh! I sat on some glue," I wail.

"I got stuck and my bum's turning blue!" Vilis shouts.

A narrow, pastoral plain backed by conical hills and barren peaks guides us toward Murchison. Forty kilometres south of the town, we enter a wooded valley where rock walls loom above us to the west. The landscape is greener here than in Canterbury, and the drive is enlivened by the rhyming game and a stream of antique cars from the 1920s to 1950s that passes us en route to some destination in the south. On the outskirts of Murchison, a lone cyclist stands at a fence beside the road, visiting with a herd of Holstein dairy cows crowded close to the fence, their long, bovine muzzles extended toward him. In Murchison, rhododendron trees no longer flaunt flaming pink blossoms like they did in September.

We stop for ice cream, and I flip through a folder titled *Murchison History* while we lick our cones in the coolness of the roadside Tip Top Café. I tell Vilis and the boys, "On June 17, 1929, a massive earthquake – the Murchison Earthquake – destroyed this town. That's the one Morgan Coleman told us about, the one that created Maruia Falls. Ten people were killed in town and seven in outlying areas. They say there would have been a lot more deaths if the town had been a major centre. The quake measured 7.8. The land on one side of a fault line was pushed up almost five metres, and the

quake was felt strongly as far away as Wellington and Christchurch."
I don't share the grisly details about families attempting to outrun
landslides that buried and killed some of their members, or the
heartbreak of a farmer watching a rock slide bury his farm and home.
"Look at this picture. It shows a huge fissure in a farmer's pasture.
And this is a road split open."

After finishing our cones, we push hard northward, hoping to
reach Motueka on the north coast before the information centre
closes. Beyond Murchison, sheer cliff faces mark many forested
slopes, and I picture rock and soil falling away as unimaginable
subterranean forces jolt the rock faces skyward. In this mountainous
country, the devastation unleashed by an earthquake would be hard
to escape.

Farther north, Kahurangi National Park stretches away to the
west, the protected area a rolling sea of forested hills extending to the
horizon. "It would sure be hard to do stoat tracking in there," Vilis
says, referring to locating radio-collared stoats using a radio receiver
and antenna, which he and the boys did during our stoat research on
North Island.

"You mean it's too hilly for good radio reception?" I ask.

"It sure is."

The Motueka Valley is broader and drier than the Murchison
valleys, its slopes overgrown by gorse and broom, its floor occupied
by brown pastures and exotic pine and eucalyptus plantations. Again,
as on our drive to Mount Somers in October, we see a hillside devoid
of living plants. The sprayed vegetation is deathly grey on one side of
a fence that separates it from a bleached, sun-scorched – but living –
pasture.

Near Motueka, pastures give way to hedged orchards of fruit
trees bearing apples, pears, and lemons, and to enclosures of kiwifruit

vines suspended on cylindrical nets. The kiwifruit plants are the first we've seen in New Zealand.

In Motueka, only a few kilometres from the enticing clear waters and sandy beaches of Abel Tasman National Park, a sign boasts the town's location in the South Island district known as NATURE'S PLAYGROUND. The boys grin. They're ready for some of that play. At the park visitor centre, we pore over a map and note distances between campgrounds as we plan our five-day tramp. A Department of Conservation pamphlet describing the track states, "In summer, the cool sea laps against safe beaches while in winter, liquid light sharpens the contrast between golden sand and emerald forests." [14] *Sounds heavenly!*

"I'll tell you right now that these three campgrounds are closed," an efficient young man working at the centre tells us as he crosses out a trio of campgrounds on our park map. "And as of Tuesday, everything north of Tōtaranui will be closed."

"Because of the fire hazard?" I guess.

"Yes," he replies.

That northern track closure will automatically shorten our tramp from fifty-one to thirty-eight kilometres over four days, not five. We'll start at the Marahau southern trailhead, as planned, but due to the closure, will finish our trek at Tōtaranui, not Wainui.

"What are our options for getting back to Marahau from Tōtaranui?" Vilis asks.

"You can take a water taxi or launch, or you can catch the bus," the park employee replies.

"We'd like to go on the water," Vilis says.

The young man looks at the four of us. "Then a launch is probably your best bet. It's bigger than the water taxis and more stable. It's less expensive, too."

"How long does the trip take?" Vilis asks.

"About two and a half hours, depending on the weather. You can catch it at any of the main bays. It stops in at different bays to pick up or drop off passengers."

Vilis purchases camping passes for four nights and tickets for the launch on Friday. Then we pile into the car to drive the last fifteen kilometres to Marahau. It's almost 5:00 p.m., and after eight hours of driving, more than anything, we all want to exit this moving vehicle and feel the earth beneath our feet.

We make camp on a grassy site beside a belt of trees shading a river in Old Macdonald's Farm and Holiday Park, which lives up to the first half of its name. Large enclosures confine numerous llamas, and smaller pens hold deer, pigs, and ducks. Chickens peck and scratch about freely, and a family of peafowl stands warily in the shadows. The domesticated birds share the campground with their wild cousins: fantails flitting among willow branches, a song thrush hopping unafraid across our campsite's grassy floor, and a pied shag standing motionless on a riverside rock, its black back a gentler curve than the rounded white rocks at the river's edge.

Dainis and Jānis snipe at each other, slinging barbed words like bullets. The confinement of our long drive has taken its toll. I put them to work setting up the tent. While our canned chilli supper heats, the river's riffles beckon, soothing my sons' tempers until soon the boys are building a dam together, their voices again light and cheerful as they lift and position rocks.

At dusk, we explore the campground. "Look at this pig!" Dainis exclaims when we stroll near a fence. "It's so *fat!*"

Next to the fence, a boar lies on grass, its head huge and heavy, its legs short projections from its bloated body. The pig's massive snout sniffs at a pile of empty corn husks beside it. My sons crouch beside the fence, wanting to pet the boar. I look at the size of its head and snout and suggest that may not be a good idea.

"Oh, he's just a pet," reassures a man who approaches from behind us. "Just a big, fat, old *kunekune*."

"Is he a *kunekune*?" I ask, recalling the small South Pacific pig at The Canterbury Show agricultural exhibition in November. "In Māori, that means 'little fat man,' " I remind the boys.

"Well, he sure *is* fat," Jānis laughs.

"Would you like to feed the pig?" An apple held in a young hand suddenly appears.

Dainis and Jānis hesitate.

"Go ahead," I say.

Dainis accepts the apple from a boy who had approached the fence while we gazed at the pig. He quickly cuts it into quarters with his pocket knife and offers one quarter to the pig.

"I wouldn't give it to him with your hand," I caution.

"Just drop it on the ground," the boy suggests.

Dainis does, and we all laugh as the *kunekune* stirs itself enough to devour the first apple quarter, followed by the others.

"Are you from New Zealand?" the boy asks.

"No, we're from Canada," I tell him. "And you?"

"I am from Germany."

We chat some more, then my family walks on. Dainis and Jānis want to pet everything, although they avoid the llamas after one bites Vilis's sleeve as we pass by.

Near the holiday park office, we see mountain bikes and a half-dozen tents spilling from a trailer hitched to a huge blue bus emblazoned with the contradictory words: THE FLYING KIWI WILDERNESS EXPERIENCE. With the campground rapidly filling up around us, it's obvious we won't be alone on the track tomorrow.

March 5

POSSIBLE RISKS: sunburn, dehydration, hunger, tiredness, get rained on, fall, get lost.

Precautions: sunscreen, lots of water, lots of food, pack light, bring raincoat, first aid kit, map and compass.

In brilliant early morning sunlight, we begin our multi-day tramp of Abel Tasman Coast Track, which Dainis has chosen as his third exploration required to earn the Explorer badge in Scouting; hence the list of possible risks and precautions.

The tidal estuary at Sandy Bay lies flat and brown, its bed of sand and gravel dissected by thin curves of aimless blue – tendrils of the Marahau River seeking paths of least resistance to the ocean. White-faced herons stalk the sands, and paradise shelducks paddle in eddies of captured blue. Like gods or prisoners, we walk above the estuary on a boardwalk, pausing often to adjust Jānis's pack. It doesn't ride his young shoulders comfortably.

AT THE MARAHAU TRAILHEAD OF ABEL TASMAN COAST TRACK

Beyond the boardwalk, which is the first leg of the Abel
Tasman Coast Track, steep-sided hills gnaw at the sky, their treed
slopes dimpled with narrow valleys. Where we enter the forest, the
track transforms into a tunnel barbed with gorse. Beech, *mānuka*, tree
ferns, and *kānuka* keep company with the invasive shrub, which
paradoxically is now recognized by New Zealand foresters as a
nursery species for forest regeneration.[15]

The trail follows coastal hillsides and is level on some
sections and gently graded on others. It offers shade beneath tree
ferns and open views of the coast. We spot Adele Island and Tinline
Bay, the latter a penetrating blue, edged with white sand beach.
Farther north, we see Stilwell Bay, where other trampers walk pale
sands toward a river pouring a sweep of thin silver into the ocean.

On reaching Stilwell Bay, we pause to munch cabin bread
(thick, crunchy square crackers) on which we spread peanut butter or
jam. The boys kick off their shoes and become children of the sand,
digging and building. They discover tube worm sculptures and a
granite Snoopy sleeping atop a shoreline rock formation, with
distinctive nose pointed to the sky.

Red-billed gulls and black-backed gulls patrol the sand, and
hermit crabs abound in shallow water near shore. One crab takes
exception to Dainis's intrusion and latches onto his toe.

"Hey!" Dainis yelps, shaking off the crab.

On the beach, a half dozen young men stand in a circle.
Laughing, they spin around, then run and fall dizzily onto the sand,
just for fun. Beyond them, their red, blue, and yellow kayaks curve up
from the sand, like smiles observing their antics.

From Stilwell Bay, the track leads us in sweeping curves along
the side of a ridge. On reaching the height of land, we trace the ridge
top northeast and angle toward the coast. At times we're exposed to

the sun's burning rays, and at other times we're sheltered within a shaded forest. After three and a half hours of tramping with increasingly sore shoulders and hips from carrying packs, we reach Torrent Bay, its sand strewn with snail and clam shells.

DAINIS ON ABEL TASMAN COAST TRACK NEAR TINLINE BAY

"This is what we came here for," Jānis says happily while he and Dainis abandon their packs to play in the sand.

Vilis and I wander over the sand, keeping an eye on our sons and the incoming tide. We urge Dainis and Jānis to don their packs, and then cross the sandy expanse to hike a final twenty minutes to Torrent Bay campsite, a collection of tent sites sheltered by *kānuka* trees. While Vilis cooks our evening meal of cheddar sausages and mashed potatoes (reconstituted from dried flakes) the boys build a sand castle complete with dikes to protect it from incoming water.

After the meal, with sand flies hunting our blood, Vilis and I erect the fabric shelter he sewed for the two of us last week, alongside the boys' small tent. Western sun caresses our sons at play in the ocean, their young limbs and chests rosy in its light. At their feet, the sand castle's dikes are breached, yet its turrets stand high and dry, as do a dozen pied oystercatchers – large black-and-white shorebirds – on a sandbar in the bay.

March 6

SUNRISE GILDS hillside forests and drops glitter onto Torrent Bay. Wasps hum among *kānuka* branches. We crawl out of our sleeping bags slowly, our legs stiff and sore from yesterday's tramp. After a breakfast of granola mixed with powdered milk and water, we break camp in mid-morning and begin our second day of tramping.

"New Zealand native forests are different from Canadian native forests," Jānis comments when we leave the beach. "New Zealand native forests are a mixture of trees all jammed together. Canadian native forests are like a stand of maple." He's thinking of the hardwood forests dominated by sugar maple trees that cloak hills near our home in northern Nova Scotia.

Surrounded by beech, *kānuka*, and *mānuka*, we drink in

breaths of cool, damp air in deep gorges, and climb to the tops of high ridges graced by pines. From the ridges, we look out over steep slopes and spot Frenchman Bay, all white sand with no more than a rounded green curve of ocean at its throat.

We tramp north through more scrubby woodlands on ridge tops and dense forests in narrow gullies. Our park map states that the gully trees provide seed stock for the regeneration of forests that were extensively logged in the nineteenth century. [16] Now the regenerating forests are protected within Abel Tasman National Park.

When we reach Falls River and step onto a suspension bridge above the dark green water, Jānis grins mischievously. "Let's all bounce up and down on it!"

The bridge is already swinging, and I envision it bucking and tossing wildly. "Let's not," I say quickly.

"Oh, come on, Magi," Vilis teases. "Where's your sense of adventure?"

"I married you, didn't I?" I retort.

He and the boys burst into laughter.

Near today's destination of Bark Bay, tall tree ferns soar against blue sky. A wide crescent beach borders the bay, and we find tent sites on a *kānuka*-vegetated sand spit. We choose a picnic table and set up our tent and shelter on a sun-dappled floor of hard-packed sand. When that's done, we hang wet clothes on a wire strung between two trees.

The boys build a sand castle. Grinning, they tell Vilis and me that they've decorated it with white shells to lure onlookers into pit traps they've dug and concealed near the castle. Then they scamper ahead of us into the ocean.

The water laps clear and sun-fractured at our ankles. We spot a sea star and small, flattened fish well-camouflaged against beige sand. Schools of minnows flash streaks of colour in the green pools of a tidal stream that rushes into the bay. We walk the stream, its bed dappled with white shells, its pools deep and cool in the day's heat. The boys invent "sink the scallop shell." They set two scallop half-shells afloat on the water, throw sand to sink them, and then set the shells afloat again. Where the water deepens, we dive, splashing and shouting, into the pool's emerald green. Chaffinches and sparrows call from the forest beside us, and jumbled shoreline boulders hold their sides and laugh along with us.

After tea Vilis says, "Well, Magi, bringing along the tablecloth was a good idea." He's referring to a plastic-coated cloth he'd grumbled about when I packed it.

"I've been waiting for you to admit that," I reply serenely.

Again, my men roar with laughter.

During the evening, small dome tents fill the campground like bright confetti dotting the sand. As we cross the estuary to check out Bark Bay Hut, the crossing becomes a game. Its aim is to step just out of reach of a gently encroaching tide that froths bubbles from crab holes and trails a haphazard train of empty purple snail shells.

On our return to the campground, we notice it's now filled with young adults, many perhaps on an OE, "Overseas Experience." No children other than Dainis and Jānis are present. While we lounge at our picnic table, a park employee brings us a sheet of paper. "It's census evening," he says.

Dainis perks up. "Oh, good! I love forms." He studies the census paper. "Listen to this question: 'What ethnic group do you belong to?' The choices are New Zealand European, Māori, Samoan, Cook Island Māori, Tongan, Niuean, Chinese, Indian, other such as Dutch, Japanese, Tokelawan. They don't list Canadian."

CAMP AT BARK BAY

PLAYING "SINK THE SCALLOP SHELL" AT BARK BAY

Vilis laughs. "Then I guess we don't exist."

"I'll put Canadian," Dainis states firmly, his quick fingers forming the letters.

Dusk creeps in like a beloved cat treading among us, its plumed tail brushing our bare limbs gently. Vilis reads aloud from William Corlett's *Tunnel Behind the Waterfall* until darkness steals type from the page.

After the boys are settled in their sleeping bags, my husband and I stroll through the campground and gaze out over darkening water that covers the sandbar where our sons had played. Flashlights bob like oversized fireflies, and a nearly full moon gleams in deep blue sky above forested peaks. The high tide surges gently against shore, and ten kayaks on the beach gleam like stranded silver fish. In my mind, I envision Māori *waka* (canoes), slim and clean-cut with upswept sterns and curling prows, drawn up on this same beach a thousand years ago under a similar moon.

March 7

SURF POUNDS onto the Bark Bay beach and draws my family from sleep. I rub herbal healing salve onto itchy sand fly bites on my feet and legs. Vilis and the boys don't bother.

After breaking camp in mid-morning, we skirt a flooded area and climb steadily through alternating stands of open *kānuka* and dense bush. We top out on a ridge and ease into a descent to the shore, and the abandoned Tonga Quarry. From an interpretive sign, I learn that massive blocks of Tonga granite were cut from the shoreline in the early 1900s. Some of the blocks were destined for the cathedral steps in Nelson and some for the walls of the Chief Post Office in Wellington.

More interested in trees than granite, Dainis and Jānis drop their packs and scramble up into stunted *kānuka*. The trees' twisted, spreading branches resemble emaciated black fingers reaching for golden sand and blue water.

TAKING A BREAK ON ABEL TASMAN COAST TRACK, BETWEEN BARK
BAY AND ONETAHUTI BEACH

Lured on by the promise of our midday meal and another early camp, we tramp a kilometre farther and step onto Onetahuti Beach, a sweeping crescent of pale sand licked by blue water and backed by green, forested hills. Again, we set up camp beneath open *kānuka* with the sound of the sea in our ears. Vilis uses a fallen branch to brush possum turds off our chosen picnic table before I spread the now-appreciated tablecloth and set out our repast: cabin bread, margarine, cheese, peanut butter and jam, dried prunes and apricots, orange drink, trail mix, and cashews.

The beach is busy with traffic. Water taxis and a red-painted launch that seats a dozen or more passengers drop off and pick up fares. Some of the passengers are day trippers who carry guitars and coolers. None are children.

ONETAHUTI BEACH

The receding tide leaves behind wet sand the colour of new rust. We find mussels ringed or tinged with lime or emerald, attached to boulders crusted and spiked with sea life. A crab pinches Dainis's hand, and we accidentally step on others hidden in the sand. One is the colour of blue-grey smoke. Several have red-and-white-streaked pincers raised high in readiness. All scuttle sideways to escape our intrusion.

Vilis steps on something hard. He brushes away the sand and uncovers a sand dollar. Its top surface is furred with soft, dull greenish-grey spines; its bottom surface is pale green with a yellow centre like the heart of a flower. Enraptured with Vilis's discovery, the boys scan the sand and shallow water and find other sand dollars, some small, some large. The echinoderms bring to mind our cranberry-picking excursions at Polly Cove on Nova Scotia's South

FINDING SAND DOLLARS AT ONETAHUTI BEACH

Shore, where we've found the bleached skeletons of sea urchins dropped onto rocks by gulls.

The beach and adjacent rocky shore yield more treasures: tubes of sand grains cemented into brittle pipes, a pink-tinted shrimp-like creature, and many hermit crabs, one of which delights us with its bright yellow eyes and antennae. I spot a cat's eye, the green and white operculum of the common sea snail *Turbo smaragdus*. An old Māori tale tells the story of two boys who saved themselves from their evil grandmother's cooking pot by placing cat's-eyes on their eyelids before falling asleep, thus fooling her into thinking they were awake.[17]

Dainis and Jānis scramble over rock formations sanded and sculpted into upward-sweeping peaks and plateaus by the tide. I ask them, "What will you miss about New Zealand when you're back in Canada?"

"Nothing," Jānis answers immediately. Since we left North Island, he's been feeling increasingly homesick.

Dainis frowns with concentration.

I tell them, "I'll miss having no bugs around our house. And I'll miss cabbage trees. And fantails." Fantails are small, perky native songbirds with long, elegant, white-bordered, black-centred tails. They inhabit wooded habitats and have become a family favourite.

"Yes," Dainis says. "Fantails."

Jānis nods. "Yeah."

Before dusk, we hike into the forest to cold green Onetahuti Pool. Its pristine, quiet seclusion is a marked contrast to the bustling campground and frequent arrivals and departures of water taxis.

On our return to the campground, we hear many languages and accents, and see many skin colours. Fluid hand movements of sign language speak for one camper. We watch a group of kayakers feast on a roasted chicken.

In the night, my runny nose prods consciousness onto me. I blast the offending snot into a wad of tissues and hear subdued surf provide background music. Other sounds intrude into the night's serenity. The boys farting in their tent. Vilis snoring. The muted thuds of possum turds falling from the trees onto the nylon shelter above me. When I'm asleep, I hear only dream sounds. The reality of being awake is so much noisier.

March 8

IN THE darkness of early morning, we fumble and pack our gear and break camp, knowing we must cross Richardson Stream before high tide invades the estuary. Fortunately, the pale beach sand enables us to see where we're stepping. Clouds blanket most of the sky except for a clear strip of pink and lavender over the hills on the far side of Tasman Bay. Much to Vilis's and Jānis's disappointment, Richardson Stream still runs low, making the crossing an easy one. "I feel cheated," Vilis grumbles.

"Yeah, this is cheap," Jānis commiserates.

On a slope high above the beach, we pick at our granola breakfast – unappetizing after four consecutive mornings of it – and look eastward into the rising sun. Then we abandon the granola and tramp on a wide, gently graded superhighway of a track that climbs to Tonga Saddle and descends toward Awaroa Bay. Cool air and spectacular views of rolling, forested hills and gleaming ocean rouse us from our sleepiness. In mid-morning, the track narrows and drops amid tree ferns to the shore of Awaroa Inlet.

EN ROUTE TO AWAROA BAY

Now we wade as we creep around land's edge, with shoes tossed over our shoulders and water up past our ankles, then past our knees.

"This is better," Jānis mutters.

The inundated trail leads us to Awaroa Hut, the Holiday Inn of huts we've encountered in New Zealand so far. Spacious and modern, the hut has large windows, an overhanging roof, and an airy veranda fronted by a half-dozen steps the length of the veranda.

While we wait for the tide to recede so we can cross the kilometre-wide expanse of Awaroa Inlet, we explore the hut's grounds, lounge in the shade of nearby trees, and read books on the veranda. Like the Māori, who are thought to have established permanent settlements on the shores of this inlet, and like European settlers who built ships, created a farm and a school, and tanned leather using beech bark here,[18] we must synchronize our movements with the ebb and flow of the tide.

WADING AT AWAROA INLET

At 2:30 p.m., more than four hours after we arrived at Awaroa Hut, clear sand at last stretches from the orange beacon on the shore in front of the hut all the way to the orange beacon on the inlet's far side. We hoist our packs onto our shoulders and strike out across the inlet, its sand strewn with shells that crunch beneath our shoes. We greet a school group hiking from the north, the children's excited voices sweet snippets of sound that peal out over the empty inlet. In the middle of our crossing, I'm struck by the disturbing thought that the tide now sliding seaward will, in less than six hours, cover this spot with water far deeper than my height. For a frightened instant, I think the tide may be capricious; however, no unexpected wall of water roars in to catch my family, far from safety.

The hum of wasps pervades the campground at Waiharakeke Bay, north of Awaroa Inlet. Although anxious to make camp, we continue on to Tōtaranui, since Jānis suffered painful wasp stings at Awaroa Hut while we ate lunch there. Wasps have been present in every campground we've camped in on this north coast.

The track parallels the coastline and descends to Tōtaranui Beach, yet another exquisite sand crescent on Abel Tasman Coast Track. For a few last hours we explore golden sand near land's end at the brink of autumn, discovering *pāua* (abalone) shells crusted with calcium deposits, sea urchins, cat's eyes, sea stars, and hermit crabs. Then we erect our shelters near a forest that stands like a tangled web at our backs.

March 9

AFTER BREAKFAST, Vilis dismantles the nylon shelter, then flips the boys' tent upside down, shaking it to remove leaves and sand. We break our last camp on Abel Tasman Coast Track and pack our lightened backpacks in readiness to catch the launch back to Marahau. Then a park employee informs us that the water of Tasman Bay, whipped by strong winds, is too rough for the launch today. Rather than enduring a pounding, two-hour ride in a small water taxi, we opt to take the bus to the southern trailhead at Marahau, where our car is parked.

Beyond the bus's windows, emerald forest enfolds us, and

sheer mountainsides fall away from the road's unguarded edges. The bus roars up steep inclines, swings around sharp curves, and plunges downhill. Within minutes, Vilis leans his head against a window, his face green with nausea. Had we known about the rollercoaster route from Tōtaranui over Awaroa and Pigeon Saddles to the feet of the Pikiruna Range, we might have braved the water taxi.

In late afternoon, the bus finally disgorges my family in Motueka. We lounge on the ground or lean on a low wood fence while waiting for the bus to Marahau. Thankfully, it arrives soon, and the last leg of our return to the trailhead is reasonably straight and mercifully short.

Dusk arrives as we pile into the Bomb, knowing we still have eight more hours of travel before we'll reach Lincoln. Soon scenery is cloaked in darkness. The night is clear, and sweet, warm air wafts in the station wagon's opened windows. At midnight, we cruise through Culverden and pass the hotel. Its door is open, and I catch a glimpse of smoky haze swirling inside the bar as Garth Brooks's clear, impassioned voice sings *What She's Doing Now* into the yearning night.

At last, Dainis falls asleep. Jānis is long dead to the world, able to sleep anywhere. Vilis and I remain on duty, alert until we reach Lincoln at 1:40 a.m.

March 10

I SHIVER as I jog home to layer a fleece vest over my wool sweater. Then I return to the tennis courts to watch Dainis play in a double knockout Lincoln Tennis Club competition that began at 9:00 a.m., more than two hours ago. He lost 6–3 in his opening set, fighting all the way, and then won in a tiebreaker. The games in both sets seemed to last forever. Now, with a 6–1 win to his credit, he takes to the court yet again in his fourth match-up of the day.

The other courts are empty. Inside the clubhouse, winners are being presented with trophies, and consolation round winners with slabs of Cadbury chocolate. Jānis and I wait and watch Dainis and Peter battle it out on the court. The only other spectator is Peter's mother, a slim woman with the muscular legs of an athlete. She and I chat, groan quietly when a good rally ends with a smash into the net, and nod in agreement when one of our sons makes a good play.

In a burst of chatter, the clubhouse empties. Players and officials stream past us. It's now past noon. Nancy Borrie, tennis coordinator, gazes out onto the court, where Vilis is officiating the set. "They're still playing! How's it going?"

"Peter's ahead four to two," I inform her. I see Dainis's energy fading. He pulls up to within a game of his opponent before losing two more to go down, 6–3.

"Well played!" Nancy calls out to the boys, then murmurs, "I think we need to get another chocolate." She quietly asks Peter's mother to drive to the store and fetch one.

Red-faced and exhausted, Dainis plods into the clubhouse and gulps down a glass of juice. Peter, looking as exhausted as Dainis, flops into a chair and receives his slab of Cadbury chocolate as the Primary Boys consolation winner.

"Well, should we go home?" Dainis asks me.

"Just wait a minute, will you, Dainis?" Nancy requests. At almost the same moment, Peter's mother prances into the room with her hands hidden behind her back. Secretively, she hands a flat packet to Nancy, who in turn presents it to Dainis. "Here's some chocolate for you, too, Dainis, because you played so well."

Dainis stares open-mouthed at the candy, then smiles in delight and cradles the huge bar of Cadbury's Country Fudge in his hands. "Thank you! I *love* these!"

Back home, I pile dirty clothes from our Abel Tasman Coast Track trek into a multicoloured mountain of laundry on the laundry room floor. A pair of Jānis's socks reeks from too many days' wear on the trail, and Vilis's cut-offs stink of mildew from being packed away wet. I throw load after load into the washer and hang them on the clothesline to dry while we finish unpacking and storing tramping supplies. Dainis drags himself through his tasks. Jānis, who's so giddy you'd think *he* was the kid who'd been awake until well after midnight, must be reminded time and again about what he's to do.

After tea, I flip through today's issue of Christchurch's *The Press*, in which there's a picture of a lone sheep standing on rocky ground that's been grazed to soil level. The background of the photo shows bleak, barren pasture of the kind we saw near Blenheim on our return drive from North Island. The caption reads: SHEEP OF THE DESERT.

This is a country of contrasts, with drought in the centre, east, and even some parts of North Island, and perennial rain in the west. When Vilis asked at smoko (coffee break) at Landcare whether we should travel first to Abel Tasman National Park or to the West Coast at this time of year, almost everyone said to go to Abel Tasman. 'It'll still be warm enough for you to swim,' was one of the comments he received. Another was, 'It doesn't matter what time of year you go to the West Coast; it's always raining there.' My curiosity is piqued. Even though we worked in what was described as subtropical rainforest on North Island, it sounds as though we have yet to experience New Zealand's true rainforests.

March 11

TODAY, AN icy wind's breath causes leaves to tremble and this old house to grow uncomfortably cool. I rise from my seat in the kitchen, where schoolbooks, homeschool journal, and lesson plans cover the table, and realize my legs are stiff from cold.

"Hello, Magija!" voices call from the hallway.

"We got on the wrong trail," Jānis tells me excitedly, his face red from the wind. "You know how Cooper's Knob has two parts? The big hump and the little lump? We ended up climbing the little one." He pauses, his lips firming with satisfied remembrance. "It was tougher than Gibraltar Rock."

"My legs are *tired*," Dainis groans, not yet having recovered from yesterday's tennis marathon.

"*Brrr!*" Vilis gives an exaggerated shiver. "There was a co-o-old wind up there, but it was good."

Hot pancakes warm us. Then my men are off to see a movie while I write. The peace of a silent house, a rare circumstance in my present existence, envelopes me gently.

March 12

ORION DANCES on his head, the night sky blazing with stars around him. Out of the northeast, a strong, warm wind blows, riffling through tree leaves. Today, it was as though summer would never end, as though the cold winds that swept across Canterbury yesterday had never been. Roses bloomed rich and lush along a garden fence. Soft warmth caressed our bare arms when the boys and I walked Lincoln's streets. Cherry tomatoes split with ripeness when pulled from the vine, exploding into sweet juice in my mouth. A new lupin blossomed, one I had transplanted as a slim, young thing with a trio of leaves. Its flower stalks now rise tall and graceful, their pink blossoms filled with the promise of summer all over again.

I felt a yearning to go back in time, like I always do at summer's end, and realized that the summer of our time here in New

Zealand is fading. The short, dark days of winter, now three months hence, will bring our adventure's end.

March 13

ROCK MUSIC reverberates throughout the Alpine Ice Sports Centre. The ice surface is freshly groomed, the glass above the boards, foggy with condensation. Coach Kim Lewis is grooving, a big smile on her face. Her bladed boots dance as she makes her entrance from the music room. Speakers blare out Billy Ray Cyrus's version of the old Nancy Sinatra hit *These Boots are Made for Walking*. It's the song Kim has chosen for Coffee Club's line dance number for the fall gala in April.

Along with most of the line dance crew from the December ice show, I'm roped into practicing the number. We start with pivots, using toe picks to rotate a half circle to the left, followed by a full circle to the left. *Pivots?* I've never done one in my life! But we don't stop there. We scull and pump backwards. We splice and do half-pinwheels. We march and do a kick line, fan out, then come together in a huge pinwheel. I stick with it and give it all I've got. The show must go on!

HOURS LATER, evening light brushes gold onto Lincoln's houses as I stroll to the Scout Hall to collect Jānis. Inside, the smoky smell of burnt wax pervades the room, a residue from the Cubs cooking pikelets (small, sweet pancakes) over their hobo stoves (cans filled with tightly rolled strips of corrugated cardboard soaked with wax). Despite the fact that it's already 8:00 p.m., the Cubs disappear outdoors for a quick game of scatterball, so I help the leaders wash and dry dishes.

That task done, I sit on a bench to wait for Jānis. Within moments, the Cubs burst into the hall.

"Pack, Pack, Pack!" Akela, Andrew Wallace, calls, and the Cubs run to form a three-quarter circle in front of him for their closing ceremony.

Jim, whose farm Jānis has now visited twice, sits beside me to wait for his son Jason. I mention that my family was away last week to Abel Tasman National Park.

"Oh, it's beautiful up there, isn't it?" Jim says.

We discuss the tracks and gorgeous scenery, and I extend my bare legs to show him my bitten ankles. "That was the first place we've really encountered sand flies. My ankles are still sore and itchy. We're planning a trip down the West Coast sometime later on, and I've heard they're bad over there."

"Well, they're just about everywhere," he tells me. "It's only here in the east that we don't get them."

"Really?"

"Yeah. They're bad in the west and in the central part, too. Around Arthur's Pass and all that area."

I smile. "So, we've been spoiled living here in Lincoln."

He grins. "I used to just hate them. They were always after me when I was younger. Now they don't bother me so much." He puts an arm around Jason, who has taken a seat beside his father. "That's because I take this guy everywhere with me. He's my sacrificial lamb. Insects would much rather bite him than me."

"Tender, young skin," I tease gently.

Jason smiles shyly.

Then Jānis is beside me, grinning, and Jim and Jason rise to talk to Akela.

"Ready to go, Jāni?" I ask.

"Yup."

"Did you talk to Akela about when you'd get the Bronze Kiwi?" This is a badge awarded to Cubs who have presented ten Kiwi Projects.

"He was busy, but I talked to Kaa (another Cub leader). He said they'd try to order it for next week." Then my son is off again, running and leaping among the other Cubs.

March 16

IN THE night, Vilis and I are jolted from sleep by the escalating roar of an engine revving louder and louder, followed by the wild scream of tires squealing on Gerald Street, Lincoln's main drag. The roar of the racing vehicle gradually fades in the distance while Vilis murmurs sleepily, "Now, *that's* hooning."

When I rise at 6:00 a.m., silver moonlight spills onto our duvet. A rose-pink sunrise softens the edge of night while I stir eggs and milk into a mixture of flour, salt, and baking powder before pouring the unsweetened batter over peach slices in a greased baking pan. I slide the pan into the oven, then take a cup of hot water to the study and write. Forty-five minutes later, the smell of peaches wafts through the house, and I rouse Vilis and the boys from their beds. Seated at the kitchen table, we flip square pieces of the baked breakfast over onto our plates and sprinkle sugar onto juicy, exposed peaches.

These are peaches Jānis collected from the gravel of our driveway yesterday, where they had fallen from overhanging branches of a neighbour's tree. When my nine-year-old brought them into the house, I looked askance at their dull skins and bruises. Some of the fruits had even split or been impaled with gravel from their fall. Yet their surface flaws deceived me, for when I halved one, I found a heart of burgundy and white, like wine and innocence and unlike the heart of any peach I'd ever seen. So, I trimmed and sliced those peaches and set them in a pan in the refrigerator to rest overnight. I knew they would lure me out of bed in the morning, in the moonlight, to bake a special treat.

March 18

ON A sunny Sunday afternoon, my family strolls the Pacific Ocean's shore near Cooper's Lagoon, about thirty kilometres south of Birdlings Flat, where we found jade pebbles in September. Flat grey stones smoothed by waves shift under our feet. The boys and I bend to collect bits of jade here, too. One piece is so smooth and oval, it resembles an exotic green egg.

Black-backed gulls speckle the shore. The adults are elegant in black-and-white plumage; the immature gulls look like grubby relatives in their mottled brown feathers. Three shags waddle away from us, the seabirds' posture upright and stilted like that of prudish old women. The shags propel themselves into the air and fly low over the shore, bodies stretched straight as arrows. My gaze returns to the stones at my feet.

"That one didn't make it," Vilis says.

"What?" I look up.

"One of the shags got knocked down by a wave."

I envision fast-flying shag colliding with incoming breaker. *Pow!* Then we see the bird bobbing to the surface beyond the surf.

Farther down the beach, Jānis adds clumps of dead grass to the slanted roof of a lean-to perched on shore above high tide. The shelter's frame is a pale skeleton of driftwood bones, its roof composed of layers of bleached grass, gorse, and kelp. A thick driftwood log serves as a seat at the shelter's entrance. "Someone had corned beef for lunch," Dainis calls out, picking up a rusted tin.

DRIFTWOOD SHELTER AT COOPER'S LAGOON

We ramble on with the earth's largest ocean roaring beside us. Near the piped outflow from Tent Burn, gulls and shags dip and dive for fish. Vilis gestures urgently for Jānis and me to run to where he and Dainis stand atop the outflow tunnel. "Dolphins!" he whispers, and we watch the arcing bodies of three dolphins cleave the water. The sleek marine mammals surface again and again as they circle and hunt in the same area as the gulls and shags. Then they're gone.

Atop the outflow tunnel, I feel the vastness of the Pacific Ocean, its waters spread before us, its handiwork of worn, sculpted shoreline behind us. Metaphors leap to mind – green soup in a bowl of stone, sprinkled with gull salt and pepper; a turquoise and mud-green sheet with one ruffled edge and one smooth edge; a South Pacific dream calling me to the tranquility of its distant horizon, then slamming me onto its shore.

This morning, flushed with fever and fighting a knock-out cold, Kim Peters, the Senior Pastor at Lincoln Baptist Church, preached from the book of Matthew. He urged each one of us to take our gifts out into the community, to salt it with the flavour of good works, to light it with the brightness of love.

Salt. Light.

As I gaze at the Pacific, it occurs to me that maybe we should be like a sparkling ocean, clear and warm, ever inviting and welcoming. Then the taste of *our* salt would be startling and tangy on the lips of those who dive into our bright depths and brush against God in passing.

March 19

THERE ARE days when children are more than a blessing, when they're lights in the darkness of what could be and echoes of all that we are. Today is such a day, with the camaraderie of brothers playing tennis before schooling, the shared longing of all of us for more as we near the end of *The Runaway Settlers*, the remarkable productivity of peaceful and focused schoolwork, the contentment of shared family chores. It's true that even when all seems dark, as with our earlier schooling difficulties, light will come.

In late afternoon, Jānis wanders in and out of the study, somehow managing to look both dejected and determined at the same time. Dainis was invited over to Josh Peters' house after school, and Jānis is feeling left out.

"I could invite Ben over," he says suddenly, halting his aimless walking. Ben is Josh's younger brother and attends the same Sunday School class Jānis does.

"You could. That would be fine."

His shoulders slump. "But what could we do?"

I stop typing and swivel to face him. "Lots of things. You could play tennis. You could show him the LEGO robotics or your remote-control truck. You could play outside in the yard or go to

Liffey Domain."

"Maybe you could call him," Jānis suggests hopefully.

"Sorry, but no."

His lips press together as he studies me. "Is that because you don't want to, or is that because you think it would be good for me to do it?"

I smile at his perceptiveness. "Jāni, I could do it in half a minute, but I think it would be good for you to do it."

He mutters, "What would I say?" and mumbles, "I don't know," before finally asking firmly, "What's his phone number?"

I look it up in the church directory and accompany him to the kitchen to prompt him with the numbers to dial. He's still torn, his feet shifting restlessly, a hand at his forehead. "Yes," he mutters, then, "No. Yes. No. Yes. No. *Yes.*" He takes the receiver in his hand and dials, in that one small motion leaping a giant social hurdle.

A short time later, dark-haired Ben appears at our door, tennis racket slung over his shoulder. He and Jānis face each other in an agony of shyness, and Jānis stiltedly suggests some of the things they could do. Ben looks blank, then says quietly, "A few hits of tennis would be nice."

They leave the house with only the odd, cautious word between them, but return with the floodgates of conversation opened and the river of interest flowing non-stop. After Ben says good-bye, smiling shyly, and leaves to walk home, Jānis flops into a chair in the study and sighs with satisfaction. "That was *fun!*"

AFTER TEA, Vilis tells me, "Today I learned some Māori protocol." He nods with new awareness. "For that team meeting next week."

"Oh, the one in Kaikōura?" I ask.

"Yeah. It's being held at a Māori place of some kind."

"A *marae*? That's a meeting place." He and I wander into the kitchen. "So, what did you learn?"

"Oh, how to do that *hongi* greeting properly."

"The one where you touch noses."

"Yes.

"So, what's the proper way to do it?" I reach up and touch my nose to his before stepping back.

"Well, you don't look down, because then you'll bump heads. And you have to be careful about glasses." He wiggles his head back and forth, as though lining up his spectacles with mine. Then he reaches out and takes my right hand in a loose grip.

"Oh, you shake hands, too?" I ask, surprised.

"Yes. And the person you're greeting will give you a signal if they want to touch noses once or twice."

"What kind of signal?" I ask.

He squeezes my hand and tugs me gently toward him. "That kind."

We touch noses again and move apart.

I smile. "Who taught you this protocol?"

"A Māori fellow who works at Landcare."

Images flash through my mind of the *marae* at Whakarewarewa in Rotorua, which we visited in late January. I envision the steep-roofed *wharenui* with its intricately carved posts and barge boards that represent a welcoming and protecting ancestral embrace. I see again the female singers' fluid arm movements and the warriors' fierce eye-rolling and tongue-wagging while they performed the *haka*. Of course, what my family saw was a concert, not a meeting. Yet even when that building was empty of singers and spectators, it resounded with the silent music of a culture a thousand years strong in Aotearoa, this "Land of the Long White Cloud," as the Māori call New Zealand.

March 20

THIS MORNING, Gerald Street's west end is lost in mist, its east end splintered into light and shadow by the rising sun. I post a letter in the mailbox next to Hammer Hardware and start back across Lincoln's deserted main street. There's peace here in the dawn, in the silence of empty streets. This peace is soon broken by starlings fighting on the bare cement parking lot in front of the fish and chips shop. One bird knocks another onto its back again and again. The victim screams while tens of other starlings call shrilly and swirl in a thin black cloud above the combatants. Perhaps they notice my presence, because the starling cloud swirls away. The victim is on its feet, and the fighters take to the sky in opposite directions.

As I stroll William Street toward North Belt, I admire the marigolds, dahlias, late daisies, and roses still blooming in Lincoln's walled gardens and along their borders. A vehicle's chugging roar announces the Meadow Fresh milk truck's turn onto William Street. The truck pulls over to the curb ahead of me, and the driver and his helper leap out and run milk bottles to gates and mailboxes. Both wear reflective clothing. The helper is younger, a teenager perhaps, with a wool hat pulled down over his ears. When the driver enters the truck cab, his helper climbs onto a running board on the side of the vehicle. Inside an open sliding door, I see crate upon crate of milk bottles, some clear and empty, the rest white and full.

My breath forms warm mist in the cool air. Above me, the sky is a motionless blue scarf stretched over the earth. A peach lies round and dark on our driveway next to two others squashed into wet burgundy masses by the car's tires when Vilis drove Jānis to skating before dawn. I glance up from the peaches to see a hot-air balloon hanging in the sky in the distance toward Christchurch. Its black, red, and yellow fabric is lit by the sun into the flaming hues of a desert in the sky. If I could, I'd be in that balloon's basket sailing high above Canterbury, rising with the sun in the freshness of this blue-scarf morning.

SLINKY AND sinuous. That's what Chris Street says the Baby Blues ice dance should look like. Kim Lewis adds that the leg movements should be slow and deliberate, as though you were pulling a ball and chain. I haven't yet mastered the correct sequence of steps, let alone given thought to making them slinky and sinuous, or like pulling a ball and chain. Yet, even if I never succeed, the attempts alone will have been worthwhile, for the challenge, for the stimulating newness. It's like Daphne, a fellow skater, told me one day after our lesson, 'The first time I came to Coffee Club, I was terrified. When I finished, I was shaking. Someone asked me if I was going to come back, and I said, "Absolutely!" ' The same goes for me.

IN MID-AFTERNOON, the boys and I cluster in the study, our hair still wet from a dip in the Lincoln University pool. Dainis composes limericks in his head while Jānis works hard to finish two he began earlier. He tosses out ideas, and he and I search the alphabet for good rhymes. I tap out beats on the desk surface, and Jānis shifts words to accommodate the 3,3,2,2,3-beat pattern. Finally, he's successful, and I type and print four limericks he composed as a Kiwi Project. Here's one of them:

> There once was a Martian from Mars
> Who liked to eat muesli bars.
> Once when he had one,

His nose turned to a bun,
Now he hides his face in the stars.

It's only after I see the limericks on paper that I realize each one contains a taste of New Zealand, whether parrot and holly, muesli bars, a Lincoln Cub leader, or today's excursion to an outdoor, unheated pool still warm enough to enjoy an autumn swim. This country is insidious. It creeps into our speech and actions, even our poetry. We'll leave it different people than we arrived, stretched and broadened without even being aware that we're changing.

After tea, Jānis and Vilis repair more of the damaged Spitfire airplane model. They carefully replace balsa wood bones, stretch tissue paper over scorched ribs, and brush dope over translucent skin. The Spitfire, like a phoenix rising from the ashes, becomes whole once more in their hands.

March 25

AT 8:15 A.M., the sun has the heat of summer, and the north breeze, the touch of a sultry lover. However, by late morning, the wind bullies instead, repeatedly shoving and nudging tall, slender shrubs near the house to bend to its will. I feel a sudden jolt and see the window frames shake in front of my desk. An earth tremor. *That* was an earth tremor! Seconds later, all is still.

I turn on the radio, wondering if a quake will be mentioned on the news. One is; however, it occurred in Hiroshima Harbour earlier this morning. While I listen for news of one potential disaster, I hear of another. A huge grass fire in South Island's Arthur's Pass area has closed the main traffic artery from Christchurch to the West Coast. I recall the dry gold of tall tussocks and parched shrubs in Porter's Pass, southeast of Arthur's Pass, when we drove to

Craigieburn Forest five weeks ago. Canterbury is desperate for rain.

March 26

A STARLING wolf-whistles at dawn's pastel pink dress. Spur-winged plovers fly overhead in formation. Calm and balmy, the morning holds the promise of heat and the excitement of newness.

We've found another home, a white three-bedroom bungalow on Maurice Street. It's far enough away from Lincoln's main drag to be considered in a quiet area, and has a small wood stove – a definite plus now that the weather is cooler. Although it doesn't have a large yard, the house is located across the street from Josh and Ben Peters' house. Dainis and Jānis are excited about that.

I harvest the last tomatoes, beans, onions, tiny carrots, and Savoy cabbages from my tangled, weedy garden. I spade up the weeds and pile load after load of uprooted plants into a borrowed wheelbarrow, then dump them onto the compost heap. The boys rake up hedge clippings strewn over the driveway, and Jānis trims back the hot-pink fuchsia, its severed blossoms like drops of bright blood on the cement path leading to our front door. This house and yard cared for us when we were strangers in a strange land. Now, as our goodbye, we care for them.

March 28

Mow. THE last of the yard work is done. *Pack.* Jānis collects walnuts from under a walnut tree he discovered in the yard's northeast corner. *Clean.* I wash the last of the windows: laundry room, bathroom, boys' bedroom. I do this for me, for my soul. *Load.* We brought so little with us from Canada and have needed so little, our second-hand furnishings like temporary friends spread around us.

Unload. Again and again, Dainis helps Vilis pack and unload the car and a trailer we borrowed from the Peters. After the last carload is packed, Dainis cycles to the library to exchange books en route to Maurice Street.

A few raindrops fall out of nowhere, startling Jānis and me. Caught between two homes, we stroll around the yard at North Belt one last time, saying our farewells to the fuchsias and lupins, to the walnut and lemon trees, to the cool blue beauty of the hydrangeas and the budding promise of the fried-egg camellia. Then we, too, ride from North Belt to Maurice Street, arriving just as rain – blessed rain! – pelts from the sky onto metal roofs, rapping out a welcome.

March 30

DISCO LIGHTS flash purple, green, blue, and red onto skaters' silver blades. Loud music reverberates throughout the rink, and teenage girls dance on the bleachers near the disc jockey's sound room. Other teens spill onto the ice until its surface is covered by a revolving mass of humanity sprinkled with a few adults and children, including the Lincoln Scout Troop. This is the Friday night public skate in Christchurch, one of the city's big social events of the week.

Since Dainis and I brought our own skates, we took to the ice and enjoyed twenty minutes of space and relative freedom before the majority of the skaters who had to hire skates joined us. But now, with the lights down and a milling mass of humanity around me, I can't even hear conversation for the loud music, and my feet are made cautious by the sheer number of skaters (over two hundred) and the occasional teenage male channelling testosterone into his blades. At last, I shrug and give up. I feel too crowded.

While I remove my skates, I listen to the disc jockey entertaining skaters. He's a pied piper to the crowd, issuing

challenges and eliciting cheers at his comments. He instructs the
skaters to change direction and later organizes races, first for girls,
then for boys. Dainis enters the boys' race and assumes the speed-
skating form he learned in Nova Scotia – body low, arms swinging,
legs pushing out long, powerful strokes – while he vies with brawnier
boys at the head of the pack. He's quiet, this older son of mine, but
the fire of competition burns strong and steady within him.

Our time in this country has thrown my family into new
situations and imposed new challenges. Some have been fun, like this
race. Others have been painful, like my sons' initial loneliness. On a
recent day, Vilis asked Dainis what he's learned during the time we've
been in New Zealand. Dainis replied that he's learned that there are
other sports in the world beside hockey and baseball, and, sounding a
bit surprised, that he likes schooling.

We came to New Zealand to explore a place far from home,
to look out over different landscapes and step out on new trails.
We've done that in the sense of this country's physical reality;
however, other explorations have been internal. Some of the different
landscapes we've explored are inside us, and some of the new trails
we've hiked haven't led us up mountains, but to new peaks within us.

March 31

WE'RE RACING against darkness. Far below, the Bomb waits in the
Blandswood car park at the foot of Little Mount Peel, a low peak on
the eastern edge of the Southern Alps' Tara Haoa Range 150
kilometres southwest of Lincoln. Almost three hours ago, we began
our ascent by following Deer Spur Track up the rumpled spine of
one of the splayed-out paws of the mountain. The track is a steep
climb to the Tristram Harper Shelter at 1300 metres, where we'll
spend the night. Each of us carries the same backpack we carried on

the Abel Tasman Coast Track earlier this month, although we've brought supplies for only one day, rather than five.

No level expanses greet us on this track. Here, we climb ever upward; first through dense native forest decorated with fuchsia trees and many others we don't stop to identify; next through alpine scrubland interspersed with flax; and lastly through moors of heath-like plants and tussocks of grass. The vegetation hugs the ground ever more closely as we climb higher. In each of the vegetation zones, sharp plants assail us, first gorse and bush lawyer, then unknown grasses with slicing-blade edges, and lastly, clumps of speargrass or spaniard with stabbing, dagger leaves.

At 900 metres, a tiny mountain lake is beautiful, its blue water surrounded by contrasting golden vegetation. Beyond it, boardwalks carry us over soggy ground, step by uneven wooden step. My leg muscles cramp into painful knots, and my backpack seems far weightier than it did on the Abel Tasman Coast Track. Jānis, who skated for two hours early this morning, romps ahead with Dainis, astounding me with his endurance.

In late afternoon, waning light heralds the onset of dusk. Vilis scans the landscape and tells me quietly, "We may be forced to sleep out along the trail."

We push on past the boardwalks and spot a small building perched high on the mountainside near the summit. Spurred on by the sight, we conquer the remaining steep incline and arrive at Tristram Harper Shelter just as light fades from the sky.

Giddy, the boys toss off their backpacks and explore the tiny shelter. It encloses little more than a table, two long benches, and a stove. Vilis cooks a dehydrated supper and then, by the faint light of sputtering candles, reads aloud from C. S. Lewis's *The Lion, the Witch and the Wardrobe*. Afterward, we unroll our sleeping bags on the two

benches and creep outdoors in the deep blue of evening to gaze at
the world beneath our feet. Cities and towns look like diamonds
studding the Canterbury Plain's velvet cloak, with Christchurch a
distant brooch flaunting a cluster of brilliant white gems at its heart.

Frigid mountain air soon drives us, shivering, indoors and
into our sleeping bags. Dainis and I lie head-to-head on one bench,
and Jānis and Vilis do the same on the other. As we wiggle about in
our attempts to find comfort on the hard surfaces, we laugh, whisper,
and pray into the darkness.

April 1

AWAKENED IN the night by Dainis's wiggling, I open my eyes to a
shelter no longer in darkness. Instead, it's infused with pink. Startled,
I sit up and stare out the window. "Vilis! Dainis! Jānis! Wake up! It's
the Southern Lights! The Aurora Australis!"

In wonder, we gaze through the window at green banners
that leap and arc across the rosy sky. Then we creep from the shelter,
stepping carefully to avoid taking a header down the mountain.
Below us, the Canterbury Plain lies peaceful, its jewel lights subdued
by the deep hours of night. High above it, yet seeming so close we
could reach out and touch its rebounding energy, a glorious light
show blazes, courtesy of the sun and the earth's magnetic fields. It
offers us a glimpse of forces so powerful we can barely imagine them.

But mountain beauty has its price. Frigid air bites, and we
shiver as we hurry back to our sleeping bags.

Hours later, Vilis calls, "Time to get up! I found the
outhouse."

The boys are cocoon-kids, no heads in sight, their bodies
amorphous bulges in black sleeping bags. Reluctantly they emerge,
metamorphosing into our shivering sons. They take turns visiting the

long drop (outhouse), which eluded us in yesterday's oncoming darkness as it's hidden by a rock outcrop.

While our dehydrated egg and meat breakfast rehydrates and cooks, Vilis reads more from *The Lion, the Witch, and the Wardrobe*, his voice faltering as he relates Aslan's slow, sad walk to the stone table. The meal bombs out, the food barely edible.

"It's disgusting," Dainis pronounces. "But the hot chocolate is good."

We abandon the abysmal meal, climb the short distance to Little Mount Peel's summit at 1311 metres, and gaze out over the landscape. A razorback ridge links the summit with Middle Mount Peel to the northwest and beyond that, Mount Peel. Ranges of long-ridged mountains roll from the western horizon like incoming waves beneath a huge and spectacularly blue sky.

TRISTRAM HARPER SHELTER ON LITTLE MOUNT PEEL

To the east, the Rangitata River flows wide and blue to the Pacific Ocean, curving and sweeping through a collage of parched and verdant, irrigated fields. We spot a falcon winging the mountain heights and a pipit bobbing its long tail up and down among low shrubs and rocks near the summit beacon.

Nineteenth-century Canterbury botanist and conservationist, Leonard Cockayne, wrote that, "Mountains are the noblest recreation ground, the finest school for physical and moral training, a source of perfect health to those who visit them, and place of all places for enlarging our minds by the study of nature in Nature's greatest laboratory." [19] On such a glorious morning, surrounded by this spectacular landscape, I can only agree.

Vilis stands atop the summit, drinking in the mountain air. As he gazes out from beneath his wide-brimmed leather hat, I notice that he's beginning to bear a striking resemblance to that "SOUTHERN MAN" I spotted on a hotel poster in Ranfurly in November. Like the poster man, he's tanned and fit, wearing shorts, standing with hands on hips, and he looks clean-cut but a little rough around the edges. All he needs to complete the picture would be a singlet, some wool socks, a horse, and a couple of working dogs.

The boys toss stones off the mountain and listen to them clatter on rocks below. Then Dainis whacks at a clump of spaniard with a dead flax flowering stalk, expecting to bash the plant's spear-tip leaves. Instead, when he raises the stalk, it's impaled on a spaniard leaf's hard, slicing tip.

We return to the shelter, pack our gear, and read notes in the hut book. One particular entry catches my eye: *8/6 Mrs. Owen's class. Great day. Stuffed children. Great to find a toilet.*

On our descent, we follow a faint spur track that plunges steeply down from the hut. On a narrow ridge, I stumble and fling out my hand to brace my fall, only to find I've thrown it straight onto a clump of spaniard. I yelp in pain and quickly yank up my hand. In my palm, I see seven neat, bloody incisions three or four millimetres wide, which fortunately don't extend right through my palm.

For three leg-jolting, knee-shaking hours we make our way down the mountain, hardly able to believe that we're travelling more slowly than we did on our way up. The boys laugh and groan about the rough track and its tough, poky plants. Their voices flare into admiration every time they spot a particular spear-bladed species growing near the track. *Spaniard.*

April 2

THIS MORNING, my sons and I dive headlong into schooling. Our climb of Little Mount Peel, with its adventures of stabbing spaniard and sky-tingling Aurora Australis, have invigorated and inspired us. In my homeschool journal, I could write, in the pattern of Mrs. Owen's comment in the hut book: *4/2 Mrs. Nams's class. Great day. Keen children. Great to find enthusiasm.*

LATER, DURING tea, Vilis asks, "Do you remember when we said there are no large native animals here?" When the boys and I nod, he says, "Well, there were. The moas."

This afternoon, my husband attended a Lincoln University seminar presented by a South African scientist who uses emu to simulate moa grazing habits so he can study plant architecture as a means of survival against moa grazing. Now, Vilis continues, "They – and I don't know how many species there were—"

"Eleven, I think," I interject.

"Yeah. They were major herbivores. And they were all different sizes. Some could graze up to three metres high! But they grazed in a totally different way than mammals do. They couldn't clip off vegetation. They had to *pull* it off. And moas couldn't push food back with their tongues the way mammals can. Like emus, they had to jerk their heads back and forth to get it to go down." Now, my husband imitates the scientist imitating an emu tossing its head back and forth while trying to swallow a strip of plant tissue. Then he eyes us brightly. "So, what kinds of things do you think would make it hard for a moa to eat a plant?"

"Small leaves," Dainis guesses while he clears dishes from the table.

"That's right! What else?"

"Tough," Dainis guesses again.

"Yes! And a lot of native plants have a different growth form when they're small than they do when they're taller. When they're young, they have smaller, tougher leaves. Once they grow past about my height – that's roughly past grazing height – they start producing big leaves." Vilis, who's six foot three, sighs wistfully. "It's such a shame all the moas were killed. You know, the vegetation now is totally different from what it was because all these introduced species graze so differently from moas."

I catch a mental glimpse of a New Zealand landscape populated by moa, from chicken size to those larger than ostriches. They're creeping through forests and swamps and pulling leaves off native plants. There's no gorse or broom or exotic pine, no roses or lupins or thyme. Then the glimpse is gone. It's too different. The invaders have encroached so far.

April 5

IN LATE afternoon, Dainis piles clothing, toiletries, and camping necessities beside his green backpack in preparation for a three-day, two-night Scout camp at Lake Daniell near Springs Junction in the north-central South Island. He'll take his pack to Scouts this evening to add troop camping equipment and have it weighed.

Excitement races through my son's words and actions, and some of it rubs off on me. As the designated female chaperone for the excursion, I'm a little nervous about the responsibility of keeping an eye on fifteen boys and girls, but am keen to tramp and bird in new territory.

April 7

THIS MORNING, cold stings Dainis's and my bare hands as we stride to the Scout Hall, backpacks on our backs. We arrive at 7:30 a.m. and greet two arrivals already there, a tall boy and his father. The boy's smile holds a mixture of embarrassment and satisfaction while his father complains loudly about the weight of his son's pack. "Why should my kid have to carry twice as much as everyone else?" The father shoves a bag of food into the top of his son's pack. "Just because he's a big boy, they give him twice as much. It weighs as much as everything else he's packed." Now, the father is trying to figure out a way to attach a plastic washtub and aluminium pot to the pack's exterior.

"I think the weights were calculated as no more than a quarter of each Scout's body weight," Dainis explains.

"Body weight shouldn't have anything to do with it. It should all be divided up equally. What are *you* carrying?"

"Four fuel canisters and a stove."

The father continues grumbling even as Aubrey, the smallest of the Lincoln Scouts, arrives carrying an old pack that bulges at its seams and protrudes from his back like a huge burl.

"Aubrey! That pack's as big as you are!" I exclaim.

He grins jauntily at me, his legs like sticks showing under the pack.

The complaining father grows suddenly silent.

At 8:00 a.m., with all thirteen Scouts, two Cubs (children of accompanying adults), and five adults accounted for, assistant leader James calls out, "So, are we sweet?"

"Yeah!" a half-dozen voices respond.

We pile into four vehicles and drive north through Christchurch, heading for Lewis Pass and, beyond it, to the eight-kilometre Lake Daniell Track. With James cornering curves like a race car driver, the two-and-a-half-hour trip passes quickly for Dainis, me, and James's two sons. Around us, arid hills are still tawny from the drought. Sunlight glints off beech leaves when we enter upland forests. Sand flies mob us in the car park at the start of the track. The beech forest we tramp through en route to Lake Daniell is cool, moist, dappled with sunshine, and blessedly free of sand flies. It's also nearly free of the sooty mould that feasts on honeydew. I see only scattered trees speckled or coated with the fungus's pimpled darkness.

Scout leader Dave Lord breathes in deeply. "Oh, it's good to be back in the forest! I just love the smell."

Albert River gleams like a green jewel as we cross a bridge above it. A few fantails and a South Island robin with a yellow blush on its chest flit down from trees to inspect us.

"Look! There's a rat!" One of the Scouts points to a grey rat hunched near a bench beside the trail. Unwary, the non-native rodent holds its ground until we're nearly upon it, then scurries into the forest.

When Dave and I stop for a moment to listen to the Scouts' chatter, he murmurs, "Get away from the radio and TV and Game Boy. Give them time for some reflection."

A few of the Scouts, including Dainis, push on ahead. Others struggle with their packs. Sarah, who carries an old, external-frame pack she obviously finds uncomfortable, stops often to remove the pack and rest before again pulling it onto her shoulders. Aubrey trudges gamely beneath his load and laughs when I boost the pack up a steep incline.

With many rests and a few stops for minor first aid, the hike for those of us at the troop's tail end, where I elect to stay so the other adults can keep an eye on the faster hikers, is a slow one. After two and a half hours, we spot Manson Nicholls Memorial Hut. It's pale green with a covered porch facing Lake Daniell. Across the lake, conical forested hills plunge to the water's edge. Several Scouts stand on a long dock, with the afternoon sunshine gilding their hair.

Once we're all accounted for at the hut, the leaders sort out sleeping arrangements. Males are relegated to a room on one side of the kitchen and dining area, and females to a room on the other side. Everyone claims a mattress on either an upper or lower sleeping platform and places personal gear next to it. I choose the bottom platform as far from the door as possible to minimize noise.

With the lake and its stock of rainbow trout beckoning, the men and most of the boys, including Dainis, grab their fishing rods. They string out along the shoreline and cast into the still water. I stay at the hut to keep an eye on the remaining Scouts, four boys and the only two girls. They're incredibly rambunctious, so I send them outdoors to blow off steam.

The fishing party returns empty-handed, and the rowdy Scouts calm down while they prepare tea. The boys and girls are required to assign tasks within their groups and complete them. Dainis is a competent camper so, instead of keeping tabs on him, I try to fade into the woodwork and respect him to handle things well.

After tea, Dave, James, and I amble out onto the dock. Moonlit reflections paint the lake surface with hills and mist; the evening air is still and silent around us. "It's so quiet," I murmur, enchanted by the scene's beauty.

"But it's a scary silence," Dave counters. "There should be moreporks calling or stags roaring."

He's right. However, there's not a single sound.

When we return to the hut, two reasons for the silence become apparent. In the light from our torches, we see movement in the grass in front of the hut and spot at least a dozen rats scurrying about. The torches also reveal possums feeding in young trees beside the hut, their round eyes startled by the light. Both of these introduced species prey on birds' eggs. Inside the hut, word races from one Scout to the next that one of the chaperones killed a possum in the wood shed with his axe, and that some of the boys killed a second possum.

Shocked, I process that information. I know possums are vermin in New Zealand, but I never expected a chaperone to kill one with an axe on a Scout outing.

James, the assistant leader, frowns. "There's a right way to go about dealing with pests. I don't think that was an appropriate action."

Outside the hut, Dainis rescues a fizzling fire by reorganizing the wood with tinder at the pile's base rather than at its top. He applies his lighter to the tinder, lays on his belly, and gently blows the flame until it leaps up into dry wood and sets it crackling. Then the boys and girls run, laugh, and cluster in the bonfire's light. They're like vibrant paintings edged with shadow.

April 8

MIST, SHOT through with sunlight, rises against green hills layered one upon another on the far side of Lake Daniell.

LAKE DANIELL

The dawn air is cold and damp, the hut behind me silent with sleepers. Intent on some early birding that I cleared with Dave, I follow a path through the forest on the lake's eastern shore. For two hours, I look, listen, and *pssh*. My efforts reward me with sightings of only four species – robin, tomtit, silvereye, fantail – plus the nasal whinnies of scaups on the water. This forest is so silent, with its sparse avian fauna. No doubt rats and possums had much to do with that.

After breakfast, the entire Lincoln Scout Troop packs food and fishing gear and sets out on a round-the-lake excursion. At promising spots, fishing enthusiasts cast lines and hooks into the still water. One of two chaperoning fathers reels in a three- or four-pound trout and displays it to admiring Scouts before returning it to the lake. Halfway around the oblong water body we picnic next to a pebble beach, and Scouts burn off energy by skipping stones over the lake.

Then we bushwhack along a faint trail on the western half of the loop, the rough hike igniting the fire of adventure in the Scouts.

"Cool!" Alyssa exclaims.

"I love this!" Dainis laughs, and he, Sarah, and Matt race through the woods, leaping over and pushing aside obstacles while they run the entire western half of the trail.

"Bushwhacking is really just following a less well-travelled track, but for some of these kids, it's their first tramp," Dave tells me.

That the bushwhacking is punctuated with minor dangers and injuries adds to the Scouts' excitement. Wasp stings. A wrenched ankle. A fish hook caught in the crotch of a boy's pants. A cut toe. These are memories in the making.

"Everybody into the lake for a swim," Dave orders after our return to the hut. "Otherwise we'll have some stinky boys," he adds softly.

Refreshed by the cold swim, the Scouts play games outside the hut. They retreat indoors when sand flies become intolerable. I rub herbal healing salve on my swelling, itchy bites and those of others who come to me asking for some of my "magic cream," as Dainis calls it. He's immersed in this camp, revelling in its varied adventures and doing more than his share when it comes to cooking and camp chores. Tea is spaghetti with Bolognese sauce, and Dainis fries mince without hesitation before adding tomato paste and other ingredients.

Other trampers have arrived throughout the day and share the hut with us. A wee girl who stepped on a wasp nest wails in the arms of her father. Word of my "magic cream" reaches the child's mother, and I offer her the salve, which she gently applies to stings on the whimpering girl's limbs and body.

After tea, the Scouts fish from the long dock, the lake peaceful as evening darkens. When night falls, they play commandos, sneaking and dashing through the clearing to break through enemy lines without being caught in the spotlight of enemy flashlights. Eventually, beds call, and silence pervades the hut.

In the night, I'm awakened by stinging pain and heat in my left foot from a particularly swollen sand fly bite. While I rummage in my pack for the jar of salve, I hear the wee girl sobbing on the platform above me. Her mother's quiet voice comforts her. Then I discern a muted, harsh, scratching and ripping sound from the end wall. For seconds I can't fathom what it is. Then, in the darkness, I realize that rats are trying to chew their way into the hut.

April 9

AFTER BREAKFAST, the Scouts lean their backpacks against the hut porch wall. Minutes later, with packs on backs, we stride into the forest. The Scouts, with their lightened loads and a weekend of tramping under their belts, complete the return hike of Lake Daniell Track much faster than the hike in. For many, it becomes a race. Dainis, Matt, Chuck, and Sarah are the first Scouts to reach the car park, knocking twenty-five minutes off Dainis's incoming time of two hours, five minutes.

In James's car, I ease off my boots. My left foot is swollen and throbbing. At Maruia Hot Springs, we soak in the hot pools for an hour before making our dash for Lincoln. The hot water feels glorious after three days of tramping and camping. It eases aches and soothes my sore foot.

Back at home, Jānis announces that he and Vilis went camping too.

"Where?" I ask.

"Andrews Stream," Vilis answers. "It's past Craigieburn Forest, towards Arthur's Pass. We left yesterday afternoon and stayed overnight. We just got home half an hour ago."

Jānis's eyes are lit with residual delight from their adventure. "We were *so* cold last night."

Dainis and I excitedly relate stories about the Scout camp. Then, with no time to unpack, we all eat, shower, and drive to the rink for *The Panoptic Experience and Ice Extravaganza*. The show opens with Māori singing and dancing, the female performers flashing white fluffy balls (*poi*) on strings, through the air. Behind the black curtain at one end of the rink, I warm up with other Coffee Club skaters, my swollen foot crammed painfully into my skate. We're third in the program and have plenty of time to practice our steps and bits of patterns. Some of the skaters grow frustrated with the long wait.

Finally, we skate through the gap in the curtains and line up in formation. Then Billy Ray Cyrus belts out *These Boots Are Made for Walking*, and our white skates flash into synchronized motion. We finish the program with details choreographed only a few days ago: eight steps, then two bubbles (sculls). Stop. Point at audience. Tip hat to right, tip hat to left. Two backward bubbles. Spin. Tip hat to audience. Rotate left arm five times in synchrony with the music's wind-down, then pull elbow back in a punchy finish. *Yeah!*

April 10

TODAY, WE have no time for anything other than unpacking from our weekend camps and packing for an Easter holiday excursion to Australia. I throw dirty clothes into the washer and hang them outside on the line to dry. We shake leaves and dirt from our packs, and pile travel camping gear on the living room floor. Tomorrow, we'll fly to Sydney, where we'll rent a pop-top van and begin a two-week exploration of New South Wales and its wild inhabitants: kangaroos, parrots, koalas, perhaps even a kookaburra sitting in an old gum tree.

April 11

MIST VEILS hedges and distant hills as we drive to the airport at dawn to embark upon our Easter vacation. The Air New Zealand jet rises and banks high over Canterbury en route to Sydney. Below us, ranges of hills and mountains sweep up from the plain like waves on a misty sea.

Millions of years ago, New Zealand, Australia, and other Southern Hemisphere islands and continents comprised the giant supercontinent of Gondwanaland. After New Zealand split away, it became a land of birds and forests. Australia developed its unique flora, now dominated by eucalyptus trees, and its eye-popping fauna of marsupials, reptiles, and colourful birds. Since Kiwis talk about Aussies with the same rivalry as Canucks talk about Yanks, our brief exploration of New South Wales may provide us with a glimpse of the Down Under version of "sleeping with an elephant."

Offshore from New Zealand, cloud blankets the Tasman Sea. On our jet's approach to Sydney, the sky clears and the flight crew informs passengers that Sydney receives 340 days of sunshine annually and is inhabited by four million people.

Bathed in its characteristic sunshine, the city sprawls across the landscape, lush with trees and twisting blue indentations that expand into bays and resemble haphazard bites chewed out of the Australian coastline. Our jet lands on a runway adjacent to Botany Bay, famous for its early penal colony and named by Captain Cook for the lush plant life surrounding it.[20]

When the taxiing aircraft makes one last turn, I spot a

Canadian Airlines jet parked at the terminal. The red maple leaf on its
tail is a sudden dagger in my heart. *Take me home!* I'm swamped by
unexpected longing to be in Canada. In this instant, I would give it all
up – the time in New Zealand, this brief exploration of Australia – to
climb aboard that jet and fly home. Here on the far side of the world,
I realize, perhaps truly for the first time, how much I love my
country.

The Sydney airport sizzles with South Pacific flavour – dark
eyes, dark skin, flashing smiles, sun-streaked hair, and tanned limbs.
So many nationalities. Vilis and I check an overhead flight monitor,
on which Christchurch and Auckland figure prominently as
destinations. Others include Wellington, Melbourne, Brisbane,
Manila, Taipei, Noumea, Shanghai, Kansai, Nadi, Bangkok, Kuala
Lampur, Athens, Vienna, New York, and Los Angeles.

"I've never even heard of Noumea or Nadi," Vilis murmurs.

"Neither have I," I whisper. Faced with world geography, my
husband and I are sadly lacking. Not so the airport McDonald's
cashier. She pegs our Canadian accents right off the bat.

We catch a train from the airport to Westmead, a Sydney
suburb. There, the boys and I watch over our luggage while Vilis
deals with the van rental. Sunshine pours down intense warmth, a
welcome change from cool New Zealand autumn temperatures. I
spot a spangled drongo perched like a black sentinel on a store roof
edge, its heavy beak jabbing the sky, its long, flared tail a sweep of
dark elegance.

In mid-afternoon heat, we head west through bedroom
communities and farmed fields and grazing land en route to our
destination: Blue Mountains National Park. In Glenbrook at the
park's northeast edge, we stock up on supplies and buy a park permit.
Then in waning light, we drive a narrow, twisting road through sheer-

walled Glenbrook Gorge to Euroka Clearing, an expanse of grassland surrounded by eucalyptus forest. Almost immediately, we spot a flock of chunky white birds with backswept yellow crests feeding in grass beside the access road.

"Those are sulphur-crested cockatoos!" Jānis cries. "And those are galahs!" He points out smaller grey-and-pink parrots among the cockatoos. His face is alight, his eyes full of wonder.

"Look over there." Vilis nods to a section of clearing beyond the parrots, where furry rather than feathered bodies feed on grass. The eastern grey kangaroos' hunched-over backs are strong, rounded curves above the roos' massive haunches and the bases of their stout, muscular tails. When one of the kangaroos raises its head and sits up, we see that its upper body is balanced on that lower tripod of power, its small forelegs delicate. One feeding roo after another balances on its tail while lifting its huge hind feet to move them a step forward.

"Look how they use their tails!" Dainis exclaims.

"Like props," I say.

"Let's park the van and walk around," Vilis suggests.

In the shadowed light of approaching darkness, the kangaroo mob feeds complacently and moves toward the forest. Handsome brown and grey Australian wood ducks also forage, unconcerned by our presence. When we turn our steps toward the van I spot a chunky, chisel-beaked bird perched on a low branch in a tree near the road. It's a kookaburra in a gum tree. My family has truly landed in Australia.

April 12

IN EARLY morning, the air resounds with raucous screeches and other unknown bird calls. I creep out of the van with my shiny, new Australian bird book in hand and discover that the screeches belong to sulphur-crested cockatoos. Noisy miners, whose black eye patches make them look as though they've been in a brawl, complain their *"pwee, pwee."* Trim magpie-larks in jazzy black-and-white plumage drop mellow notes or call stridently from low trees. Crimson rosellas – slim red-and-blue parrots – take my breath away as they wing silently from one tree to another like vibrant maidens eluding ardent pursuers.

In the midst of this noisy avian activity, eastern grey kangaroos tail-prop their way slowly and silently through the clearing while they feed. One female, carrying a joey, pats her pouch gently with a forepaw.

EASTERN GREY KANGAROOS AT EUROKA CLEARING

AFTER BREAKFAST in the van, my family sets out an early morning hike – a bushwalk if we're "talkin' Strine" – on Bennett's Ridge Fire Trail. Smoke taints the air, and slender eucalypts bleed red resin or flaunt scribbled patterns on their bark. Banksia shrubs, named for the wealthy botanist Joseph Banks who sailed with Captain Cook on the

Endeavour, bear fruiting structures that resemble tiny corn cobs.

Fantails and silvereyes flit through the open woodland, and a male rose robin with a pink and white chest flies from one low perch to another. In a burnt-over section of forest, trees are black skeletons in a charred wasteland. Only a half-burnt clump of a spiny grass the boys christen "pins" protrudes from the earth. The rest is blackened earth and ash.

After four hours of hiking through the open gum woods, Dainis complains, "It's all the same."

"Think of something to do," Vilis suggests.

Our twelve-year-old rummages through his pack and finds an extra pair of socks and a long piece of string. He cuts the string into two equal lengths, balls up each sock and ties it to one end of a string, then swings the socks into the air. He grins. "These are my pois." The socks flash up and down and trace intricate patterns while Dainis whistles along the trail back to Euroka Clearing.

KATOOMBA. THE name is a low flute tone, the town itself the focus of tourism in the Blue Mountains area. At the Echo Point visitor centre, Australian king parrots eating fruit at a feeder dazzle us with their scarlet and green plumage. Inside the centre, I ask a park interpreter what we need to know about poisonous snakes and whether it's safe to go off tramping.

"There are poisonous snakes out there, but they're uncommon," the personable young man assures me. His accent, surprisingly, is not Australian. "When I moved here from the States, I worried about snakes, too. But I've done a lot of bushwalking, and I've never seen a snake in the wild. I'd *love* to see one."

"So, we don't need to take any special precautions?" I ask.

"Not really. Just use common sense."

"Like no bare feet when you're walking around the campground?"

He nods. "No bare feet. Keep your shoes on."

We stroll to the viewing site at Echo Point and gaze out over the Blue Mountains – a seemingly endless expanse of densely forested, steep-sided ridges and plateaus. Exposed sandstone escarpments and deep gorges offer evidence of thousands of years of erosion. A high rock formation called The Three Sisters stands like a trio of guardians overlooking a sea of blue-tinted air. That air is laden with vaporized eucalyptus oils, which cause the bluish hue and inspired the name "Blue Mountains." The wild part of me wants to abandon this tame viewing spot, hike through the forests below the escarpment, and search for platypuses in rivers. The practical part of me tells me that's not why we've come to Australia – this time.

HOURS LATER, hairpin curves in the darkness challenge the van's grip on the road while we search for Old Ford Reserve and its campground in Megalong Valley, west of Katoomba. In the shifting pool of light cast by the van's headlights, we spot the pale flash of a kangaroo hopping away in a field, and then a sign warning:

KANGAROOS

WOMBATS

HORSE RIDERS

DRIVE CAREFULLY

At length, we arrive at the campground, too exhausted to eat. After visiting Echo Point, we drove to Katoomba's Maxvision Cinema to view *The Edge*, a movie about the Blue Mountains, displayed on a six-story-high screen. As we prepare for sleep, my minds is filled with images that make me want to leap into adventure.

THE THREE SISTERS, BLUE MOUNTAINS NATIONAL PARK

April 13

IN MID-MORNING sunshine, we head out on another bushwalk, this
one an exploration of Megalong Creek, which runs through Old Ford
Reserve and the campground.

Loathe to leave a small fire he's built, Jānis asks, "Is this
going to be a more interesting walk than yesterday's? That was like
the TransCanada Highway of walks. It was all the same."

"It'll be very different," I assure him. "Much shorter, and
we'll stroll along the creek."

Appeased by the lure of water, the boys join Vilis and me in a
leisurely exploration. They leap from one exposed rock to another,
the tea-coloured creek, shallow and still around them. Thick riverside
forest echoes with the tinkling calls of bell miners, the birds' olive-
yellow plumage bright among dark leaves. Female superb fairy-wrens
– their tails cocked upward and dusted with blue – flit like grey-
brown sprites from riverbed rocks to shrubs at the water's edge.
Behind them, the forest is dull green and backed by the eroded cliffs
and plateaus of the Blue Mountains.

After a quick lunch at the van, we drive to Govett's Leap
Lookout north of Katoomba. From the viewing platform, the "leap"
or waterfall is visible as shining silver tresses spilling far beyond a cliff
edge surrounded by barren rock faces and forested valleys. As we
hike from the lookout toward Pulpit Rock, three yellow-tailed black-
cockatoos fly overhead. Lemon-yellow "windows" of feathers in the
cockatoos' tails resemble sails lit by the sun.

Where the track passes beneath a looming sandstone bank
curved like a concave lens, we pause to read names scratched into the
soft rock by countless visitors who – perhaps realizing their
insignificance in comparison with the magnificence and scope of the
blue-tinted landscape that rolls and climbs to the horizon – felt

driven to leave some sign of their passing.

Dainis searches the trail's edge. "Is there a stick here somewhere?"

Seconds later, I glance over my shoulder to see him stretching tall, stick in hand, his arm high above his head as he scratches his name in among the others.

After the day's explorations, we return to Old Ford Reserve, lit by campfires in the darkness. Beside one fire, a pregnant woman dressed in pink and black stands bulging in golden firelight while a scruffy-bearded man sings to her in Italian. Again, Jānis gathers sticks and builds a fire. Its embers glow in the darkness while my younger son sits close, reading unknown stories in the spurts of flame and incandescent coals.

April 14

KANGAROO. OMNIPRESENT eucalyptus. Southern Hemisphere.

As we drive north from Old Ford Reserve, we play our road trip end-letter, beginning-letter word game, with the proviso that all words or phrases must relate to Australia, and with the amendment that a new word may start or end with the first or last letter of the previous word.

Platypus. Summer's too hot. Torresian crow. Wallaby. Low. Wombat.

Mist spreads an eerie blanket in narrow gorges alongside dark, damp Megalong Valley Road. Eventually, the gorge cliffs give way to views of clouded valleys. North of Blackheath, we travel east. After consulting our map yesterday morning, Vilis and I realized that Australia is so large (almost as large as Canada) that we can't hope to explore the Outback – Vilis so much wanted to do that – during this short Easter vacation. So instead, we decide to drive a loop through national parks from the Blue Mountains northeast to Dorrigo and back again.

Sulphur-crested cockatoo. Omnivore. Echidna.

A red fox lies dead on the road, its crushed body, gory evidence of Australia's troubled history of introduced species. Red foxes were first brought to this country from Europe in the mid-1800s for sport hunting and later to help control the population explosion of previously-introduced European hares. Highly adaptable, the red fox has spread throughout most of Australia and is considered likely to be the sole factor in the extinction of dozens of species of native Australian mammals.[21]

INVASIVE SPECIES IN AUSTRALIA

Like New Zealand, Australia was isolated for millions of years and developed its unique fauna as a result. Australian animal life is highly susceptible to non-native predators like the red fox, feral cat, and cane toad (an insect pest control attempt that went horribly wrong). Australian native animals are also susceptible to habitat destruction and competition for food by introduced non-predator species such as rabbits, hares, and feral camels, pigs, goats, horses, donkeys, and water buffalo. In short, like in New Zealand, introduced species in this country have created an ecological nightmare.[22]

Australia. Eastern rosella. Ants. Sunshine three hundred forty days a year.

We skim along a rock ridge that descends steeply on both sides of the paved road. Open gum forest borders the pavement through Blue Mountains National Park, but unexpected apple orchards and clearings edge the road near Bilpin, where chunks of agricultural land are sandwiched between Wollemi National Park to the north and Blue Mountains National Park to the south.

Red birds. If you want to drive across Australia, it's very far.

From Bilpin, we turn north toward our destination for the day – Singleton in the rich grazing land of Hunter Valley. At Bulga, we drive past hay fields and pastures, the latter supporting small beef herds and a large dairy herd. Near Singleton, we see a vast open-pit coalmine in the distance. According to my guidebook, the mine is one of several in the area. Apparently, Singleton is booming from the combined wealth of mining and agriculture.[23]

Outside Singleton, we pause near a freshwater pond so I can do some quick birding. Australasian grebes – small, yellow-eyed diving birds – and dusky moorhens similar to New Zealand's *pūkeko*, swim among stems of dense pond vegetation. Welcome swallows patrol the pond's surface for insects, and an immature spotted turtle-dove perches on a dead branch atop a tree. A male superb fairy-wren – with head, throat, back, and tail painted in bold blue and black by an unseen cosmic artist – flits from branch to branch in a stand of eucalypts and pines. I add four more "lifers" to my species list.

New South Wales. Superb fairy-wren. New Zealand's smallest island.

In Singleton, we pop the van top in a caravan park – an expanse of green lawn broken by pads of cement and brown-painted cooking shelters and shower houses. A nearby tawny hillside is graced with tall, wide-crowned gum trees growing in a spacious arrangement, as though the warmer temperatures here to the north of the Blue Mountains have induced broader, more relaxed growth.

Very hot sun. New Zealand's west island. Doo-doo from dingo.

After making use of the shower and laundry facilities, we explore the caravan park. I spot flocks of roosting European starlings in trees – they resemble dark clouds. Eastern rosellas perch on branches and fences, their vivid plumage like jumbled rainbows. These two species could be poster-birds for Australia's ecological dark and light – invasive species vs. native species.

Dramatic landscape. Eucalyptus trees. Euroka Clearing. Grey kangaroo. Galah. Hobart. Firth. (I think you mean Perth.)

In the wee hours of night, Vilis sneaks about within the van and plants Easter eggs for our sons while midges bite his and my bare feet in the darkness.

April 15

A LAUGHING kookaburra's demented chuckles invade the dawn. My sons scramble through the van looking for treats, their laughter as sweet as the music of songbirds. Outside the van, dew evaporates quickly in heat that hits us head-on before 9:00 a.m.

"This is Australia, Magi," Dainis reminds me.

Outside Singleton, green and gold rangeland erratically tufted with eucalyptus trees stretches kilometres into the distance, ending at the feet of wooded hills piled against the sky.

RANGELAND NEAR SINGLETON, NEW SOUTH WALES

We drive north to Scone, the "Horse Capital of Australia," and scan the town's surroundings for horse-filled pastures and the town itself for ice cream signs, neither of which are apparent. Vilis laughs. "In New Zealand, we would have seen three dairies already!"

"Maybe all the horses are back in the hills," I suggest.

"Could be," he agrees. "Cooler there."

North of Scone, herds of beef cattle speckle hilly rangeland. Some of the missing horses graze in tree-shaded paddocks. A ploughed field lies black and rich in the heat of the sun.

The highway tells many tales. Kangaroo roadkill speaks of danger in the night. Pickup trucks whisper poems of vast open spaces and country life. Countless white vehicles hint at the rewards of reflection in a land dominated by the sun.

North of Murrurundi, where the Great Dividing Range's wooded hills thrust themselves into the sky, fleets of cumulus clouds race to the horizon.

Vilis gasses up in Wallabadah. "This is a real farming town," he says. "That gas station I went into could be anywhere, and that café could be anywhere." Then he adds, "Maybe twenty years ago, anywhere."

Beyond Wallabadah, the highway leads us over rolling plains grazed by sheep and cattle. Trees are sparse, the cattle drawn to their shade. Vilis shakes his head. "And to think this is autumn."

Wallabadah. Murrurundi. Katoomba. I'm struck by the sounds of these place names. They roll off the tongue, the vowels repeated and soothing, so unlike the equally vowel-laden *Tongariro, Kaikōura,* and *Te Ānau,* wherein the shift among sounds is crisp and bold. How much does a people's language reflect their character? Were ancient Aboriginal Australians peaceful and submissive, those qualities seeping into the sounds that issued from their lips? Did the warring Māori do battle even among the syllables of the words they spoke?

The sun beats down. In the Peel Valley town of Tamworth, which heralds itself as the "Country Music Capital of Australia," we pause to picnic in a park. Cantaloupe juice drips from our hands. We hear no music and feel only heat.

I blow out a breath. "Whew! I can't imagine what it must be like in summer, working on the land."

From Moonbi Lookout, the view is one of rich, valley-bottom farmland. To the north, exposed granitic bedrock and stranded ridge-top boulders called *erratics* tell a story of past glaciation. We push on beyond Kia Ora Station and through a dry, rolling plain with scattered trees. A cluster of Lombardi poplars drops yellowed leaves onto dry grasses, reminding me of the drought-stricken trees in Canterbury.

"You don't see many cars carrying mountain bikes or kayaks or yuppie adventure things like that," Vilis comments.

In Uralla, we stop at the Driver Reviver Station for coffee, lemonade, biscuits, and conversation. "You've come here at the right time, with our low dollar," the attendant, an older woman, tells us before pouring lemonade for the boys and me. "Cooler now, too." She passes Vilis a cup of coffee. Her accent, like those of the other Aussies with whom we've spoken, is softer, not as biting and stretched as Kiwi accents.

The highway leads us on. Armidale. Wollomombi. As the van climbs into wooded hills on the edge of the Great Dividing Range, clouds pull together into grey quilts. In oncoming dusk, we reach Ebor Falls and drive onto a rough track beside a cattle pasture.

Adjacent to the pasture, open woodland is flamboyant with avian blossoms: pink-and-grey galahs, black-and-white magpies, brilliantly hued crimson and eastern rosellas, brown-and-blue kookaburra.

"There's a kookaburra," I point out to Vilis and the boys.

Jānis smiles and asks me, "Is it in a gum tree?"

"It is."

My sons and I sing *Kookaburra Song*, and Vilis kicks in harmony. Then my husband opens his bible and reads the Easter story while Australian dusk settles around us.

April 16

LIKE A cleaver splitting a lush fruit, the track we parked on last evening splits our world into two realms. We have the wild exoticism of parrots in the mist and the fenced domesticity of beef calves destined for slaughter.

After the boys awaken, we drive to nearby Ebor Falls picnic area in Guy Fawkes River National Park, where patches of sunlight warm the cool, humid air.

UPPER EBOR FALLS

While I prepare breakfast, Dainis perches on a barricade post in full sun, book in hand. Jānis attends a small fire he built in a fire pit, using sticks he gathered last evening. We feel at peace. The open, subalpine forest of snow gums and black sally beckons us to walk endlessly. The dull roar of Ebor Falls repeatedly draws us to the edge of a cliff alongside Guy Fawkes River. In trees at the cliff top, male and female red wattlebirds flutter warily from branch to branch, a droplet of pink flesh (wattle) dangling from their cheeks. In morning mist, Ebor Falls gleams like a necklace of silver strands tossed over the edge of a rocky table seen through frosted glass.

After sunshine teases away the mist, we stroll upstream to Upper Ebor Falls. Guy Fawkes River curves serenely through gentle slopes and open woodland before it reaches the falls. Then it roars over a black cliff, its waters pounding down over basalt columns – both the cliff and columns are remnants of a volcanic eruption eighteen million years ago.[24]

In late morning, we drive out of the dry hills surrounding Ebor Falls toward our destination for the day, Dorrigo National Park and its rainforest, 50 kilometres to the east and 550 kilometres north of Sydney. When we descend out of the hills, the highway leads us through lush farmland framed by tall shelterbelts, populated by dairy herds, and composed of red soil like that of Canada's Prince Edward Island.

The town of Dorrigo is quiet on this Easter Monday. Our presence seems to cheer the Four Square Discount Supermarket cashier and the national park receptionist. We picnic outside the Dorrigo Rainforest Centre in the park and laugh at Australian brush-turkeys that skulk at the rainforest edge and race across open lawn surrounding picnic tables. The black-feathered birds are the size of small turkeys and sport bare red heads and necks, as well as unusual, sideways-flattened tails. Behind them, the rainforest exudes the aura of a wild animal, crouched and waiting.

When we enter the forest, a yellow carabean tree dwarfs Dainis and Jānis as they tuck themselves into recesses in its massive trunk. The tree's leafy canopy is fifty-five metres above the ground, higher even than that of the giant *kauri* Tāne Mahuta in New

Zealand's Waipoua Forest. As we follow the Wonga Walk rainforest path to Crystal Showers Falls, we meet other woody strangers identified by interpretive signs: tamarind, with its yellowish bark and feathery leaves; fragrant and furrow-barked sassafras; flame tree, which in spring or summer sheds its leaves and instead is cloaked with red flowers; and red corkwood. Palms in the forest understory spread fronds in the dim light, and a yellow-throated scrubwren with a black mask chitters in dense shrubs next to the path.

Vines thicker than the boys' legs lure them upward, hand over hand, until they stand on the buttressed roots of forest giants. On his descent, Jānis snags his clothes on a thorny creeper and calls, "Hey, I've found something that's even worse than bush lawyer!" Two hikers on the trail glance over their shoulders at him.

Clumps of cunjevoi or native lily, with huge, spade-shaped leaves, grow alongside the path's lower reaches. The focus of our hike, Crystal Showers Falls, is a fine spray of sun-touched silver. It dives elegantly over a cliff that looks like a child had piled stone blocks and decorated them with cascades of ferns. We skirt a round blue pool at the falls' base, and the boys exclaim with delight as the track leads us behind the waterfall. At our backs, an overhanging rock face forms a slanted wall. In front of us, a thin curtain of falling water screens our view of the trail we descended.

When we return to the rainforest, Jānis looks around at the towering trees and muses, "You know, trees have a kind of magic. They drop this thing called a seed that's two millimetres by one millimetre—"

"There are some a lot bigger than that," Dainis interrupts.

Brotherly quibbling ensues.

"Okay, trees drop a seed that's whatever size," Jānis concedes, "and it takes water and nutrients and sunshine and such things and transforms them into something entirely new."

Vilis picks up the topic. "Mostly what they use are carbon dioxide and water, and that's what they produce when you burn them."

"They produce water?" Jānis asks. "Oh, yeah, I guess they're juicy. So, they take carbon dioxide and water and magically transform them into this magnificent new structure, which when you burn it, produces more carbon dioxide and water!"

Vilis laughs. "That's right."

I gaze at the rainforest, so rich with life, yet once called "scrub" by settlers, according to park information. In 1986, the astounding wealth of subtropical plant and animal species within Dorrigo National Park's rainforest received international recognition as a World Heritage Area.[25]

As darkness approaches, we leave Dorrigo to return to the national parks near Ebor. Mist envelopes the van and shrouds the landscape as we drive upland through the rainforest. At last we emerge onto a range of open hills just as sunset flames across the sky beneath a parasol of magenta clouds shot through with tangerine. In the distance, silhouettes of umbrella-crowned gum trees and beef cattle look like miniature black lace figures.

April 17

SMOKE WAFTS from our campfire as the boys lounge before the flames. Morning sun paints strips of tawny brown and shadow-black across a picnic site at Barokee Rest Area in Cathedral Rock National Park. We're a few kilometres southwest of Ebor Falls and once again my family is at peace. I watch a New Holland honeyeater feeding in campground gums, the small bird's body all streaks and patches of white and black, its white eyes bright in its black mask.

Refreshed and relaxed, the four of us set out on Cathedral Rock Track, a circuit around a massive granite outcrop. The first section of track leads us through boggy heathland and into open subalpine eucalyptus forest. The air is cool and sweet. A white-throated tree creeper tosses bits of bark down as it forages for insects, its long, curved claws anchoring it to a tree trunk while it climbs upward. At our feet, lanceolate eucalyptus leaves lie dusty brown on the forest floor.

Yesterday's walk through damp, lush rainforest is no more than a tangled memory of sultry sensations. Instead of cunjevoi, we encounter grass-trees with leaf blades flaring out into globelike structures, as though they were fountains within this dry, upland forest. The flowers of banksia shrubs resemble tufted corncobs or thick yellow candles. On one banksia, a male eastern spinebill – a sleek brown and grey honeyeater – dips its long, curved bill deep into flowers to feed on nectar.

Halfway around the circuit, we take a side track that leads to Cathedral Rock. Soon we encounter granite columns and gigantic moss-covered granite balls in the forest. Like strangers from the earth's past, some of the rocks resemble tall, bulging men wearing stone hats. Others look like giant marbles. Dainis and Jānis duck behind a spherical boulder and peek out, their blond rounded heads miniature reflections of the rock's curves. Close to the heart of the outcrop, we creep under massive boulders wedged onto others and use twisted, braided shrub trunks as handholds to pull ourselves up between the tons of rock looming above our heads.

"There's a chain!" Dainis calls from beyond the last shrub. He scales the next stone obstacle with the chain's assistance, and the rest of us follow him upward onto the top of the outcrop. All around us, granite curves into barren heights. Dainis lounges on a rock throne.

JĀNIS, DAINIS, AND GRANITE BOULDERS NEAR CATHEDRAL ROCK

From our vantage point, we can see forested hills and valleys that stretch to the horizon, as well as more of the hulking, jumbled mass of the outcrop – blocks, towers, balls, and massive spheres of granite. In the distance, white puffy clouds float on pale blue sky to the hazy horizon. Two huge wedge-tailed eagles soar dark and broad winged above the forested valley, their long tails resembling feather diamonds trailing in the wake of their wings.

We scramble down through rocky crevices and retrace the trail to the circuit track. Near the rest area where our hike began, I spot a wallaby in a heathland clearing. It's smaller than the eastern grey kangaroos we saw at Euroka Clearing. It's also a different colour – grey and tawny with rust at the base of its ears and a pale stripe across each cheek. "Look!" I whisper to Vilis and the boys, and we all freeze.

That we've stumbled across this macropod (kangaroo family)

while on a casual hike reminds us that this is *real* Australia, not a zoo. We're south of Wallace's Line, that hypothetical barrier that coincides with a deep ocean trench separating islands of the Malay Archipelago. Wallace's Line marks a zone of separation between Australasian and Oriental faunas. Generally, placental mammals live to the north of that line, and marsupials (pouch mammals) and monotremes (egg-laying mammals – the platypuses and echidnas) live to the south of it.[26] Even though we saw kangaroos at and near Euroka Clearing, it's this wallaby that makes Wallace's Line seem real to me.

WHEN THE sun drops toward the western horizon, we drive to nearby Thungutti Camping Area in New England National Park and buy a permit to spend the night. In the oncoming dusk, we drive to Point Lookout. From the edge of the Great Escarpment that rears 1564 metres above sea level, we gaze out over forested hills that seem to stretch forever. Distant farmland – the coastal plain – is a thin band on the far side of the forested hills. Tomorrow evening, we'll camp on that plain.

We leave the cliff edge (also formed from ancient outflows of basalt from Ebor Volcano[27]) and stroll paths through a stunted Antarctic beech forest. Two female superb lyrebirds skulk in the forest's grassy understory. Like wild turkeys or pheasants, the lyrebirds slip easily through the vegetation, their long tails flowing behind them.

April 18

IN THE dim light of early morning, eastern grey kangaroos are hunched shadows feeding in clearings as we drive away from Thungutti Camping Area. Today, we leave the upland Guy Fawkes

River, Cathedral Rock, and New England National Parks to descend through rainforest to the Pacific coast.

Once more, the eastbound highway takes us from upland eucalyptus forest through farmland to the Dorrigo Rainforest Centre. At the centre, we step onto the Skywalk, a trestle-supported, railed boardwalk that ends in a viewing platform high above the ground. At tree-top level, we soak up the warmth of early morning sun, sharing its heat with a male regent bowerbird – gloriously flamboyant in its regal dress of orange-yellow and black – and with a Lewin's honeyeater – far more subdued in its grey plumage highlighted by a pale yellow half-moon behind its bill. In keeping with its colouring, the bowerbird erupts into short, eye-catching bursts of flight that carry it from tree to tree, while the honeyeater forages surreptitiously in the rainforest crown.

After a picnic breakfast, we drive through tangled rainforest out onto cleared, lush agricultural hills. A white-faced heron and a large flock of Australian white ibises forage in pastures beside the highway – the ibises look as though their bills and bare heads were dipped in pots of India ink. We link up with the coastal highway and drive south, pausing to gas up in the quiet town of Urunga. As we cross a bridge, I spot a great egret in the river below – its purity of stillness belies the lightning speed with which it attacks prey.

At Nambucca Heads, surfers and body surfers ride waves onto the pale sand of Beilby's Beach. Captivated by the sight, we pause in our travels to give it a try. The ocean is surprisingly warm and gritty with sand that peppers unprotected skin. It actually hurts to get hit by a wave. We fight to get our timing right to catch crests and ride them in. Vilis and Dainis are far more adventurous than I am, and they swim well beyond my reach. I keep an eye on Jānis, who, after riding a wave into shore some distance away, shows signs of struggling in the water. Hastily, I swim, then wade toward him. My legs soon feel the sucking power of a current carrying me in his direction. Grabbing him, I pull him with me parallel to the shore until we're free of the rip.

"Are you okay?" I ask.

With his eyes huge, he replies, "Yup."

"Let's head back this way, to safer water." When Vilis and Dainis join us, I warn them about the rip current.

After we leave the beach, we drive slowly through Nambucca Heads, a picturesque resort town at the mouth of the broad Nambucca River. "Hey, those are rainbow lorikeets!" Jānis exclaims. He points to small parrots flying above the street, their bodies vivid collages of green, blue, red, orange, and yellow feathers. In Bellwood Park, we lunch in the shade of tall trees, with heat sizzling around us. Other picnickers lounge at tables or play in the river shallows under the glaring sun. The heat doesn't seem to bother them. Three Australian pelicans cruise over the water, and an assortment of water birds – little egret, pied oystercatcher, pied stilt, spur-winged plover, silver gull – share the open feeding ground of the river mud flats.

When Vilis suggests it's time to move on, Jānis and I abandon the shade for a quick parrot hunt – we want to see as many as possible! Drawn to raucous screeches emanating from a small tree, we study jumping leaves until we spot a scaly-breasted lorikeet manoeuvring from branch to branch. Its green plumage is almost invisible among the leaves, and the yellow, crescent-shaped "scales" on its breast are like a series of small waves rolling onto an emerald shore. My son and I grin at each other.

SOUTH OF Nambucca Heads, flat coastal plain stretches toward Jerseyville and Hat Head National Park, our destination for today.

Cattle egrets feed among beef cattle near Macksville. Near Jerseyville, debris caught high on pasture fences attests to recent flooding.

"Last flood was two weeks ago," we're told by an elderly man at the information centre in Jerseyville. Here, buildings are perched on stilts. They make me think of a community of tree houses without any trees.

April 19

IN HAT Head National Park near Jerseyville, green birds flash in trees, and green fish flash in a tea-coloured river. High in a tall tree, a whistling kite – all shades of blonde and brown – perches near a bulky stick nest. In the clear, green-tinged ocean nearby, small fishes are slivers of darkness. By 8:30 a.m., the temperature in the campground soars into the upper twenties.

We leave the park and drive south along the coast toward Port Macquarie, where we'll visit a koala centre. Dairy herds graze in lush pastures beside the road, and drowned corn crops and grasses stranded on fence wires provide more evidence of the recent flood. Near Kempsey, drier, more wooded land surrounds us, and farther south, fire damage on trees is evident. Port Macquarie, with its palms trees, pastel-painted houses, and bird-of-paradise plants flaunting brilliant orange blossoms, exudes the atmosphere of France's Mediterranean coast.

We locate Billabong Koala and Aussie Wildlife Park just outside town and make our way to the koala breeding centre. Inside, we're allowed to touch the soft, thick fur of a female koala seated on a rail fence. The koala rests on its rump and clings to a fence post with all four feet. Each of its feet displays a two-three split of toes, and each toe has a sturdy, curved claw. Tufts of long white hair bush out from inside the koala's ears, and its black nose pad forms a shining curve above pink lips.

"How old is she?" I ask the keeper, a gentle man who moves with quiet confidence within the koalas' enclosure.

"About nine years old," he says.

Vilis caresses the koala's grey and white fur. "Her pupils are vertical like a cat's."

"Well, they are mostly active at night," the keeper tells us, before moving on to let others pet the koala. Minutes later, he returns. "I'll just bring her back for one more pat. She has a joey in her pouch."

AT BILLABONG KOALA AND AUSSIE WILDLIFE PARK

Dainis's and Jānis's eyes light up, and they touch the koala tenderly. Dainis rubs its chin, like he rubs his cat's chin at home in Nova Scotia.

"How old is it?" I ask, referring to the joey.

"About two months."

"How old will it be when it comes out?" Vilis asks.

"About seven months." The keeper carries the mother koala to a feeding area, then plucks a smaller koala off a fence and begins talking to another group of visitors.

Dainis listens in and whispers, "The man said they don't have a tail, but that they have a really hard tail bone so they can sit on it all day." Interpretive displays also inform us that a female koala's pouch is a rear-facing one, and that a joey spends about six months inside its mother's pouch, followed by six months on its mother's back.

Many koalas in the enclosure slumber in crotches of artificial "trees," three of their clawed feet clinging to the wooden poles, and one foreleg hanging limply. Other koalas move about slowly, stretching their long forelegs forward to grip a railing or pole, and then shifting their short hind legs forward. One koala on a fence rail clutches a leafy eucalyptus branch in its fist and raises narrow, pointed leaves to its mouth.

Outdoors, kangaroos and wallabies wander the lawns between wildlife enclosures. Some scratch. Others rest. One boomer (male kangaroo) has a torn ear and injured foreleg – likely wounds sustained while battling another male over a breeding female. Vilis and Dainis pat the friendliest of the roos and feed them puffed rice we bought at the visitor reception desk.

Jānis holds out his hand to offer rice puffs to an emu gobbler in an enclosure. The huge, flightless bird's finely divided feathers drape over its body like a soft black and grey stole. Its muscular neck ripples as it bobs its head back and forth. It plucks the rice puffs from Jānis's raised palm, much to my son's delight.

Other native birds, including parrots, are enclosed in aviaries and large cages. One is a sulphur-crested cockatoo that tolerates our appraisal and offers a few politely enunciated English words. As we walk away, it roars a shattering screech at Dainis, who jerks in terror at the sound. Afterward, the cockatoo emits rough, raucous mutterings, like chuckles following a good joke.

We leave the koala centre and drive south to Diamond Head campsite in Crowdy Bay National Park, approximately halfway up New South Wales's slanted coast. Here, surf booms onto a beach adjacent to the campground. Kangaroos feed among colourful tents, and a white-bellied sea eagle wings over the shore, carrying prey in its talons. For an hour before dusk, we play in the ocean. As we return to the van, darkness settles in and a kookaburra's crazy laugh rips into the night.

In the pop-top van, Jānis looks up from a book he's reading. "You know, writing was an amazing invention. To think that someone puts these little black marks on paper, and hundreds of years later, someone else comes along and reads them and knows what he was thinking." He pauses before also telling us, "You know, I've realized it's better to not always be thinking ahead to things, but to just think about what's going on right now."

I study my younger son's face, recalling how anxious he was before skating in an ice show in December. "I think you're right. That's an important thing to know."

"What have you learned about Australia?" Vilis asks him.

"Well, I've learned that kangaroos look like what I always thought they did, but I didn't know they use their tails to walk."

I say, "I've learned there are over six hundred species of eucalyptus trees, and that koalas eat the leaves of only two or three of those species."

"Four," Jānis corrects me.

Dainis adds, "Netball and rugby are Australia's national

sports."

"And there's a National Surfing League," I say.

"We don't see all the yuppie bicyclists that we do in New Zealand," Vilis adds. Around us, the van feels close and cozy, like a tent. Its screens allow in warm evening air and sounds of the Australian night.

April 20

THIS MORNING, heat is a burning kiss on bare skin, the sun brilliant in a clear blue sky. I say, smiling, "This gives us a little taste of the Australian sun. And it's only eight-thirty!"

"And we're not even in northern Australia," Vilis adds.

"And it's not even summer," Jānis tags on.

The Diamond Head Loop Track leads us through heathlands and wind-contorted shrubland to exposed Diamond Head. Here, waves in Crowdy Bay smash against a red rock arch, and white-backed swallows dip and soar past sheer cliff faces.

It's too hot to linger, so we hike quickly to the shady shelter of the woodland near our campground, where golden-brown leaves litter the forest floor. The scene reminds me of open maple forests in Nova Scotia. In fact, I'm so lost in its beauty that an object on the trail ahead doesn't register at first. Then I distinguish black scales laced with pale yellow, a flicking tongue, and a flattened, muscular body. A lizard, larger than any I've ever seen, rests motionless on the trail only ten metres ahead of us. We freeze.

"What's that?" Jānis asks.

With a burst of reptilian speed, the lizard lunges off the trail and sprints two metres up a tree. As though someone flicked a switch, it freezes into stillness, its flattened head directed toward us.

We step slowly toward the reptile to observe it. "Don't go too close," I caution the boys.

"What kind of lizard is it?" Dainis whispers.

"I don't know, but it's beautiful," I reply.

"And fast," he adds.

In a spurt of movement, the lizard climbs higher into the tree and out of sight.

Farther along the trail, we meet a park employee and mention our lizard sighting. "It was one and half metres long!" Dainis tells the black-haired, bare-chested man, who is driving a small trail-packing machine. "We saw it right near the camp."

"Oh, that fellow." The park employee grins. "That's a lace monitor. It's a member of the goanna family. He'll race right up a tree and then stare down at you with his beady eyes."

Dainis nods. "It ran right up a tree."

"It was BIG!" Jānis tells the man.

"Oh, there's an even bigger fellow that reaches seven feet. It's called a perentie."

"Around here?" I ask.

"Yeah. In open areas."

"Where would you go to look for that big lizard?" Vilis inquires.

"Campgrounds and other clearings. You might not see one for two months, then you'll see three in the same day." The man shares a few more tips and drives on.

Back at our campground, we hurry to the beach and allow breakers to crash over us, washing away the day's heat and sweat. All around us, kids on surfboards or wearing flippers attempt to ride the churning waves to shore. I tell Vilis, "The water here is so much warmer than the ocean around New Zealand."

"Yeah," he says, floating on a wave's crest. "People think

New Zealand and Australia are right beside each other, but most of Australia is closer to the equator than New Zealand is."

Hungry, we return to the campground. A young girl stands within its dappled shade, captivated by a cluster of kangaroos. A boy in wet swimming trunks tosses a hotdog to a two-metre lace monitor crouched motionless in the dust. I find the huge lizard's presence near our van unsettling, as though it were a conduit to a time when reptilian giants ruled the earth. I can almost feel their essence seeping up through the dust of this campground into the monitor's scaled legs and oozing out through its unblinking eyes.

In afternoon heat, we drive south from Crowdy Bay along the coast and pause to stretch our legs at an expanse of sand dunes near Mungo Brush Campground in Myall Lakes National Park. "Evil mozzies," Dainis mutters, swatting at mosquitoes that swarm around us.

"Aussie mozzies," Vilis laughs. "Come on, let's run up and down those sand dunes!"

Grins flicker on the boys' faces, and we yell and guffaw as we scramble up the face of a ten-metre dune, its sand sucking at our feet. Then we race down it in giant sliding leaps, laughter tearing holes in our travel-weariness. Refreshed, we continue our drive.

When darkness creeps in, we pop the van top in Mungo Brush Campground. Then we lie flushed and sweating in Australia's autumn darkness. We're 200 kilometres north of Sydney and wishing for the Blue Mountains' coolness. In the night, flash after flash of lightning flares in the sky, the storm too distant for the sound of thunder to reach our ears.

April 21

A KOOKABURRA'S insane laughter and the hum of mosquitoes beyond the van's screens awaken us. Humidity saturates the air, and clouds darken the sky. Radio reports tell of severe storms in Sydney overnight. Flooding. Trees down. Lightning strikes.

After breakfast, we drive south through Myall Lakes National Park, and then continue to Hawks Nest with the hope of spotting koalas in the Koala Zone of a reserve that juts into the Myall River. We scan the reserve's tall eucalypts for plump, slow-moving bodies or motionless grey lumps in tree crotches, but see none. Still, it's good to know the koalas are there, beyond our vision.

South of Hawks Nest, we drive in rain through farmland that gives way to forested hills cloaked in mist. Here, the four- to six-lane Pacific Highway is blasted out of sheer red and brown rock. Traffic thickens forty kilometres north of Hornby, a Sydney suburb, and in the distance, the broad silver-grey Hawkesbury River opens to the Tasman Sea.

IN LATE afternoon, mist hangs in the forest surrounding Euroka Clearing, to which we've returned for the sheer vibrancy of its life. Light rain dampens the fur of kangaroos and urges it into wet spikes. Sulphur-crested cockatoos pull up grasses with powerful grey beaks and thick tongues, their young beside them begging for food with low, guttural hisses. Occasionally, the air is shattered by the same raucous cockatoo screeches that sent Dainis jerking in terror at the koala park in Port Macquarie.

Umbrellas in hand, we hike a short trail through dripping forest to Nepean River. The riverside woodland is far lusher than the nearby open gum forest through which we hiked on Bennett's Ridge Fire Trail nine days ago. Here, trailing plants cascade over rock steps strewn with yellow, orange, and brown leaves. Yellow-flowering shrubs border the path. "It's like a lush garden," Vilis murmurs.

"Those leaves almost remind me of Canada," Dainis says.

We stroll through thick vegetation alongside the river, but don't linger – the rain is more insistent, and daylight has begun its slow parade toward dusk.

Back in the van, I notice blood running down my right leg. "Must be a bite of some kind," I mutter. Then I spot a dark, elastic body writhing on the van floor. "*Ah*. A leech."

I discover two more bites on my left leg and two more land leeches in the thick cuff of one of my discarded socks. No doubt, the blood feeders were hidden in the dense, wet plants growing alongside the river. I envision them squeezing their anterior suckers between the elastic fibres of my sock cuffs and then attaching the suckers to my skin and piercing it with their teeth. When I pulled off my wet socks, I also ripped off the leeches, interrupting their meal and leaving a trail of blood on my skin.

"Better check your legs, too," I tell Vilis and the boys, and they take a look but don't find any leeches.

I reach for the salt shaker.

Jānis cries, "But the salt will kill them! I don't want you to kill them!" Far more compassionate than I, he collects the leeches, carries them out of the van, and releases them in the wet grass to seek another potential meal.

April 22

At Taronga Zoo in the heart of Sydney, a platypus swims and dives tirelessly within its tank, its grey leathery bill like a prosthesis attached to the sleekly furred body of a graceful water mammal. In a much larger tank, sea lions swim and dive, their nostrils opening or closing as the marine mammals alternately surface and submerge in their pool while we observe them from behind clear glass panels. We're envious of their fluid movement, of their grace. Bored elephants pace rhythmic dances in their enclosure, and a Komodo dragon – pale green and startlingly immense – rests within its shelter in cold-blooded stillness that reeks of menace. Rain pours down. Free-flying Pacific black ducks wing overhead. My family huddles under a table umbrella near a concession booth, the boys drinking vast amounts of Coke simply because refills are unlimited.

As the rain abates, we discover the Skycar and ride it repeatedly up and down over the zoo forest. Afterward, we check out more Australasian fauna, learning on our last full day in Australia that this country is home to eleven of the world's fifteen most poisonous snakes, a fact much less disturbing to learn upon exiting a country than when entering it.

In an amazing coincidence, Vilis meets a former student of his from the Nova Scotia Agricultural College. The two of them eye each other furtively near the emu enclosure until the young man steps forward and asks hesitantly, "Dr. Nams?"

"Hello!"

The young man grins. "I didn't expect to see you here."

Vilis laughs. "I didn't expect to see you here either."

They chat for a few minutes before we leave the zoo.

As dusk approaches, we board the Sydney Harbour ferry to return to the train terminal downtown, after which we'll ride a train to Westmead and return the van before booking into a motel. On the rocks below the zoo, a male darter (also called a snake-bird or anhinga) tips its daggerlike beak to the sky and spreads its wings to dry – its body is all curves and kinks of black, grey, and white.

The ferry ride is peaceful, the rain exhausted. Like treasure escaped from imprisoning clouds, sunset over the harbour flashes molten gold onto glass-sided skyscrapers. It gilds the Sydney Opera House's white sails the instant before a flock of doves flies beneath the golden shelter to roost for the night.

April 23

ON THE train from Westmead to the airport, my sons' voices are loud and young in the quiet crowd of adults commuting to Sydney. One of our fellow passengers is immersed in a rugby newspaper; another reads a Chinese newspaper. Beyond the train windows, young palm trees grow slim and tousle headed in new plantings alongside the railway. A huge blue and white poster proclaims:

EXCUSE ME FOR NOT SHOWING UP AT WORK TODAY

I FELL INTO A BEAR'S CAGE

At the airport, airline symbols decorate jetliners like scarves and pendants worn on graceful white necks: Japan's JAL with swirling pink flower and red bird, Australia's Qantas with a roo, Air New Zealand with a stylized Māori spearhead. From the air, the parked jetliners look like stiff-winged swans floating on concrete under the baking sun.

ON THE far side of the Tasman Sea, New Zealand is a slim girl awash in blue, with South Island's West Coast forming a lush green fringe interrupted by rivers escaping the Southern Alps and braiding through forest and farmland to the sea. Beyond the snow of the Alps, dry mountains and hills roll onto the Canterbury Plain. That familiar plain looks so neat and organized, now brown and colder with autumn present in bare branches and discarded leaves.

April 24

LIKE DUSTY fruit dipped in washing water, we're plunged back into the lives we've made in Lincoln. Jānis skates in the darkness of early morning, a sea away from New South Wales's colourful parrots – my favourites being the red-and-blue crimson rosellas.

Later, I skate with the Coffee Club group, my skin reintroduced to cold after the scorching Australian heat and warm northern Tasman Sea – so much warmer than New Zealand's waters, even those of North Island and Abel Tasman National Park.

After a morning of art instruction with the boys, Vilis inline skates to Landcare, freed from the constant demands of driving Aussie highways. The sheer bulk of Australia is staggeringly larger than New Zealand. During our travels, our kids had jokingly referred to Australia as "New Zealand's west island" and "New Zealand's smallest island."

During the afternoon, Dainis and Jānis return library books and post letters – quiet, familiar tasks that release travel burdens leaning on their young souls. While Dainis loses himself in new fiction far from Aussie mozzies, Jānis takes up pencil and crayons to create drawings of the eight Australian parrot species we observed, which he'll present to the Cubs this evening, as a Kiwi Project.

Later, when Akela asks the Cubs who should present the first Kiwi Project, the Cubs chant, "Jānis! Jānis! Jānis!"

April 25

THIS MORNING, I drink in cool, clear air and bright sunshine as I stand outside the school entrance in Springston, awaiting the start of the Anzac Day parade and memorial service in which Lincoln Cubs and Scouts will participate. Dainis and Jānis are hanging out with their Scouting friends, and I chat with Akela Andrew Wallace. "In Canada, we have the equivalent of Anzac Day on November eleventh," I say. "It's called Remembrance Day. In Tatamagouche, the village near where we live, the weather is invariably windy and cold on Remembrance Day, and we usually have rain or sleet or snow. It suits the mood of the day, but it's nice to have good weather for a change, here."

"Yes. We are usually blessed with that here," Andrew comments. "So you have your day in November?"

"Yes, because the First World War ended on November eleventh."

Our discussion is interrupted by the arrival of a huge sand-coloured truck from Burnham Military Base. It pulls up beside us and disgorges soldiers dressed in green-brown camouflage. Girl Guides in pale turquoise fleeces and navy skirts also arrive and form clusters of blue-hued flowers among the earth-coloured soldiers and Cubs and Scouts clad in dark green.

"Are your parades well-attended?" Andrew asks.

"Yes. Always." I look about me. "And you have a good turnout today."

"Yes. There's renewed interest the past few years. Ten years ago, there would have been only half a dozen of us standing around here and maybe six soldiers."

The Cubs, Scouts, Girl Guides, and soldiers take their places in the parade, which is led by a piper, a member of the New Zealand Scottish Regiment.

After the parade, I hear the New Zealand national anthem, *God Defend New Zealand*, for the first time in a small public hall:

God of Nations at Thy feet
In the bonds of love we meet
Hear our voices we entreat
God defend our free land.
Guard Pacific's triple star
From the shafts of strife and war
Make her praises heard afar
God defend New Zealand.
Ev'ry creed and ev'ry race
Gather here before Thy face
Asking Thee to bless this place;
God defend our free land.
From dissension, envy, hate,
And corruption guard our state;
Make our country good and great,
God defend New Zealand.

A former air force navigator presents the keynote address to the group gathered within the hall. He mentions that he trained in the Canadian provinces of New Brunswick and Prince Edward Island, causing me to realize that the links between this country and my own are so much stronger than I ever imagined. Even the piper who led the parade was almost a mirror image of the piper who leads the annual Remembrance Day parade in our Nova Scotia village of Tatamagouche. This, then, is the legacy of the Commonwealth, that union of far-flung nations formerly governed by Great Britain.

April 26

FICKLE CHILDREN. Yesterday, on an autumn afternoon bright with sunshine, I had to order Dainis and Jānis to spend time outdoors –

they were hardly able to tear themselves away from new library books. Today, they've spent the entire afternoon outdoors, and when I ask them to come in to do house chores, they groan and complain, "You're ruining our afternoon of outside fun!"

I tell Vilis about their fickleness when he arrives home from work.

He laughs. "That's good. Not that they don't want to do chores, but that they don't want to come in."

I agree. Our sons have become real townies here in Lincoln. And yet, some days they yearn for the space we have on our old farm in Nova Scotia, and for our forest. One day recently, Jānis stated firmly, 'One of the first things I'm going to do when we get home is to go out in our woods and built a little fort that nobody else knows about.' Another day, Dainis told me, 'I'll be glad to have more space when we get home, and to have my tools and LEGO.' Then he quickly added, 'But I'll miss doing errands. And going to the library every second day.'

Weeks ago, when we tramped Abel Tasman Coast Track, the boys were hard pressed to think of anything about New Zealand they would miss after we return to Canada. I think they might be surprised. I think we might all be surprised.

April 27

TODAY IS a day out of time, a summer dream-day tossed in with autumn's grasping coolness. At the Lincoln University tennis courts, I'm one of a dozen women walloping three backhands in a row over the net at our coach, Chris, and then increasing my agility by dancing three-steps over a black-and-yellow training ladder stretched out on an adjacent court.

"What a glorious day!" is proclaimed again and again. In a

voice filled with dry amazement, Nancy Borrie adds, "And there's no wind! Put a mark on the wall. Here we are in Canterbury *and there's no wind!*"

"When you come right down to it," Chris tells us, "tennis is all about movement. You should be able to get to most of the shots. As I've said, I'm a hundred and two, and *I* can still get to most of them, so you should be able to."

Ready stance. Lunge for the short one. Plant feet. Topspin. Follow through. I haven't forgotten. The joy of physical challenge surges through me.

IN LATE afternoon, Vilis and I attend a special tea at Landcare Research that features Sri Lankan foods cooked by a Landcare researcher and his wife. When we arrive, the coffee room is awash in corduroys and jeans, jerseys and rugby shirts, casual hair styles and the distinctive lack of concern for fashion prevalent among wildlife biologists the world over. Glasses filled with drinks gleam in relaxed hands, and eastern aromas spice the air. The meal features deep-fried triangles of light bubbly dough that melt in the mouth, a mild chick-pea and spinach dip, long green beans laced with a tangy sauce, deep-fried fish balls, braised potato chunks, rice, and small pieces of meat in a peppery sauce that's so hot my face is flushed and my nose drips.

I only recognize a few faces, so stick close to Vilis, laughing when he introduces me to Jean, a woman from New Brunswick who graduated fifteen years ago from the Nova Scotia Agricultural College. "We lived in Australia for seven years," she tells me. "When we moved to New Zealand, I felt like I'd come home."

"Because of its similarities to Canada?" I ask.

"Yes."

English-speaking. Commonwealth. Mostly temperate climate.

Analogous landforms. It's as though this country is a slender sister long ago departed for the deep blue sea on the far side of the world, yet ever waving.

April 28

DAINIS TURNS to me with a puzzled look on his face. "What are they saying? It sounds like 'Get a drink.' "

My family is watching the second half of the Canterbury Crusaders vs. Durban Sharks international rugby match, and the crowd at Jade Stadium is chanting. I tilt my head, listen carefully, and then translate. "They're saying 'Canterbury,' but pronounce it 'Kent-e-bree.' "

"Oh!"

"Magi, I can't figure out what they're *saying*," Jānis, who is seated on my other side, mutters in frustration.

I repeat my explanation.

"Oh! Well, I wish they wouldn't be so loud."

Around us, the chanting spectators – adults and children – wave red-and-black pennants and tube balloons. They wear red-and-black hats or scarves or a red coat and black scarf. On a huge, brilliantly lit field below the stands, men uniformed in red-and-black, striped shirts and black shorts and stockings sprint across unbelievably green grass. Their rivals are suited out in grey and white.

So, this is footy. Rugby. New Zealand's national sport. There are end lines and goal posts as in American football, which is called "gridiron" here. The ball is a white pointed oval similar in shape to a football. It's kicked and passed and carried, and the aim of the game is to transport the ball over the opposition's end line and then "plant" it. This usually entails taking a dive onto the grass and ramming the tip of the ball into the turf. The passing, however, is only backward or to the side. The tackling is much less aggressive than in gridiron, and there are scrums and mauls during which the ball disappears into a cluster of players, then spurts out somewhere to be snatched up by a vigilant player and moved downfield. With the exception of an occasional soft helmet or elastic thigh pad, the players wear no protection against the frequent collisions and tackles they endure. One Crusader was removed from the field on a stretcher in the first half of the game, and so far in the second half, two others have been less seriously injured. The game appears to be first and foremost one of speed, sprinting, and leg power.

"Magi," Jānis enthuses, "were you watching the playback screen when it showed the South African team up close? Did you notice how *big* their thighs are?"

The players dash. They leap into the air to catch the ball. They hoist a team mate high to catch a pass thrown in from the side line. They never give up, and the ball changes hands and teams countless times before a score is made or a referee's whistle blows.

"So, what do you think of rugby?" I ask Dainis.

"I like it. It's better than baseball." Then he adds quickly, "But not better than hockey."

"Yeah, this is more interesting than watching baseball," Jānis says wearily, "but I'm getting bored."

Exhausted is more like it. I exchange glances with Vilis, who with Jānis rose at 4:50 a.m. to be at the rink in time for Jānis's 6:00 a.m. skate. Add to that the excitement of having four boys over for Jānis's birthday party this afternoon, and the sum is a ten-year-old who can barely keep his eyes open.

With the Crusaders ahead 34–24, we leave our seats and make our way down through the stands, pausing at the entrance level to catch the last seconds of play before the Canterbury fans go wild.

Outside the stadium, we dodge horse manure dropped by the mounts of a half dozen "Crusaders" who circled the playing field prior to the game to the tune of Vangelis's majestic song *Conquest of Paradise*. An inflated, mounted "Crusader," obviously custom-made, slowly deflates as we walk by. The brown horse sags to the ground, and its rider, dressed in a red tunic with a white cross, follows it in a nosedive.

In the car, away from the noise of the stadium, we compare notes on the game.

"I *liked* it," Vilis states. "It seemed like a real New Zealand kind of sport."

Dainis comments wistfully, "It looked like it would be fun to try."

I say, "I was really surprised at the way the crowd booed the Durban team when they came out onto the field."

Jānis grumbles tiredly, "I wish that kid behind me wouldn't have been so loud and liked kicking the backs of seats so much."

On a tangent, I toss in, "Do you remember when we saw the really bright lights from Little Mount Peel and thought they might be the lights at Jade Stadium? Well, Dainis and I figured out from the schedule that the Crusaders played the Hurricanes in Christchurch that evening, so it probably *was* the rugby field's lights we saw."

A little of that evening's magic sifts into the air. It dusts us with memories of a tiny shelter perched high on a mountain, of a plain sparkling with lights below us – the really bright ones those of Jade Stadium – and of a pink sky dancing with green banners of the Aurora Australis.

April 29

THERE'S NO space. The trees are too close. Although I would run this narrow trail through Bottle Lake Forest Park with perfect ease, it terrifies me on a bicycle. Vilis and the boys race ahead and easily dodge obstacles. I ride in frozen fear – and wipe out twice. The second fall bruises my right arm and shoulder, so I give up and pedal instead along a quiet gravel road through the park.

The evidence of forestry is everywhere. Neat rows of young pines surround me and create a collage of plantations of various ages. In Pre-European times, this land north of Christchurch wasn't forest at all. It was part of a vast swamp that stretched from the sand dunes south of the Waimakariri River to the shores of Lake Ellesmere. The local Māori of the Ngāi Tahu tribe gathered foods, medicines, and fibres from the swamp and counted on the vast wetland barrier to deter attacks by raiding tribes arriving from the coast.[28]

After European settlement and the purchase of land from the Ngāi Tahu in the late 1840s, things began to change. Settlers tried farming, but soils were poor and the swamp claimed many cattle. The city of Christchurch bought the land in 1878 to use as a disposal site for sewage – "night soil" – and toxic wastes. Soon after, sylviculturists experimented with planting exotic trees. Their trials revealed the remarkable growth potential of a Californian pine species – *Pinus radiata* – in New Zealand's climate. The list of uses goes on – military training ground, piggery during World War II, current landfill site, commercial plantation, and popular recreation area.[29]

"That was awesome!" Jānis cheers when we drive away from the park.

Dainis shrugs. "It was okay."

I say, "It's not my kind of thing."

"But I thought mothers could do anything," Dainis teases.

His comment prompts laughter from all of us even while my

arm and shoulder ache.

WHILE VILIS pulls off his inline skates, he puffs, "I just had a very intense morning!"

"Analyzing data?" I ask in surprise.

"No. With possums. I spent the morning massaging possums' bottoms with a glass tube to get them to pee, then shoving the tube in the right place under their tails to collect urine samples. And all the while, the possums were going–" He hisses and snarls at us. "And the technician was saying, 'Now, don't let them bite you!' "

"Why were you collecting urine samples?" Dainis asks.

"For a study about sterilizing possums. We had to wake them up and pull them out of their bags before we rubbed under their tails." The possums were housed in outdoor pens at Landcare Research and had access to burlap sacks attached to the pen walls by hooks.

"*Bags?*" the boys ask in unison.

"Yeah. Bags," Vilis tells us. "That's what they sleep in. And they *were* asleep. They didn't like being woken up."

I can imagine. Possum sterilization, particularly if such a measure were to be implemented through aerial drops of drugged baits, could be a lifesaver for New Zealand's forests and birds. If the research yields positive results, the silent hills surrounding Lake Daniell may once again resound with the night calls of moreporks.

I have no energy. Instinct tells me to rest, to restore my injured arm and shoulder. "I guess mothers can't do everything," I quip to Vilis.

He grins. "Yes, they can. They can even fall off bicycles."

POSSUM IN BAG AT LANDCARE RESEARCH

May 1

TODAY'S DREARY sky is like a darkness of the soul – the drizzle that drips onto the earth, like tears of God. I'm stiff and sore from my fall, but glad to be back on the ice. Kim Lewis introduces my skating group to forward three turns. She changes direction from forward to backward on one foot while her blade describes a neat "3" on the ice. A sudden fear of falling besieges me, fluttering from within on frantic wings. Again I'm on a trail too narrow – this one a blade of steel.

DURING THE afternoon, Jānis reviews his Māori counting from one to ten and recites the numbers in six other languages: Latvian, German, French, Japanese, English, and American Sign Language. Then, with his mind filled with the seductive sounds and movements of language, he romps to the Scout Hall and presents his multilingual counting to the Cubs as his seventeenth Kiwi Project. He's shooting for twenty and the Silver Kiwi Badge, and would continue on for the Gold Kiwi Badge, except that we'll leave this country before he can complete the additional ten projects.   .

May 2

TODAY, THE boys and I race through schooling, one subject handing the baton to the next. Then we dive into preparing chocolate desserts to share with Andrea and Andy this evening. I bake a cake. The boys dip banana slices, walnut halves, and marshmallows in melted semi-sweet chocolate to create homemade chocolates, and Dainis pieces together a box of marbled chocolate before decorating it with chocolate leaves.

While our creations cool, I drive Jānis to the Alpine Ice Sports Centre for his afternoon skate. For the first time, as I sit high in the stands and watch my son practice his jumps and spins, the rink seems a foreign, lonely place. *It's time to go home.*

Six weeks ago, when Christchurch's vegetation was tinged with the colours of early autumn, I told Vilis, 'I'm glad we're going back to Canada, where the seasons are so distinct.' Lost in a blue mood, I was contrasting Canada's pronounced seasons to the gradual, almost imperceptible blending of seasons in Canterbury. 'But I'm glad we've lived here. It's been good.' Then I had a disconcerting thought. Could it be that even with all our adventures and explorations, I might be homesick? I immediately dismissed that idea.

That's for the boys. Yet I recalled a moment when both Jānis and I so looked forward to being at home in early July – in time to pick strawberries and cherries, then Saskatoon berries and raspberries, blueberries, blackberries, and apples.

DURING THE evening, laughter and conversation fill the house when Andrea and Andy join us for tea and chocolate treats. Our conversation ranges from Air Force World and Ferrymead Historic Park to Little Mount Peel and the Crusaders' match against Durban.

"Why is Anzac Day held on April 25?" I ask, after mentioning the boys' participation in the parade last week.

"Gallipoli," Andy answers. He explains that thousands of soldiers from New Zealand and Australia died at Gallipoli, Turkey, on April 25, 1915. He sets the scene: a hill overlooking a beach held by Turks and Germans, a British commander ordering troops onto the beach, the subsequent slaughter on that first day of the months-long, unsuccessful Gallipoli campaign. He tells us that blame for the slaughter was laid on the Brits' possession of old, inaccurate maps. I recall the plaques I saw on Witch Hill in early November, and the fact that a number of the fallen soldiers' deaths were linked with Gallipoli.

"What does Anzac stand for?" I ask.

"Australia New Zealand Army Corps," he replies.

"They were called the Anzac troops," Andrea adds.

Restless for action, my sons slip away. They return to the dining room carrying a laundry basket filled with water balloons that shimmer like oval bubbles of a glistening rainbow. Andrea's eyes light up, and we dash outdoors to form pairs of balloon tossers. Shouts of laughter resound as we toss the water-filled projectiles back and forth, ever farther and higher until they splat against our hands and surroundings with satisfying wetness.

May 4

TODAY, THE Port Hills are lost in clouds so dense and grey they could be smoke. Drizzle speckles the car's windshield, and puddles lie on pavement. The desperate dryness is gone, the drought broken by days of cooler temperatures and gentle rain. Pastures are greening at last, and paddocks are filled with grey-woolled sheep. In three months' time, Mount Bradley Walkway and other Canterbury tracks will again bear signs stating "TRACK CLOSED DUE TO LAMBING."

YESTERDAY, WHILE Dainis sat on my bed and spliced one end of a rope, I was driven to organize, to make lists of tasks needing to be done, as if we were leaving New Zealand tomorrow. In one frozen moment at the rink two days ago, I realized that I'm no longer only here. Part of me has already abandoned this country, if only in thought. Our time here is a cup rapidly filling with sand. Every day, every minute, the sand grains push higher and higher until no space will remain. Then my family and I will slide over the cup's lip into the space that's the future beyond Aotearoa.

May 6

THIS MORNING, the world is green and silver, grass and mist. Drizzle soaks my tank top and shorts while I run. It blur fields and hedges lining Ellesmere Road outside Lincoln. Sheep appear as rounded grey shapes in paddocks washed with rain-soaked shades of green. A livestock trailer parked by the roadside and crammed with sheep reeks of lanolin and manure – thick, biting smells hot against wet air.

DURING THE afternoon, while Dainis skates at the Alpine Ice Sports Centre with his Sunday School class, Vilis, Jānis, and I explore downtown Christchurch. Outside The Arts Centre of Christchurch – a complex of elegant grey stone buildings originally built to house girls' and boys' high schools and Canterbury University College, but now devoted to the arts – we chew caramel hazelnuts bought from a smooth-talking vendor, one of many with tables and booths set beneath a sky grey with the threat of rain. Woodworkers offer bowls and wee sets of drawers shaped from *rimu* and *tōtara* wood. Other vendors sell sheepskin slippers and woven wool socks, handmade soap, pickled ornamental peppers, stone statuettes and jade jewellery, fudge, original watercolour paintings, and light-catchers formed from copper wire and clear marbles.

After wandering through the market, we amble down Worcester Street past the perimeter walls of a construction site painted with sharp-edged, futuristic designs in rainbow colours accompanied by indecipherable writing. Elsewhere all is grey: grey sky, grey streets, grey buildings. Still, the greyness is soft, companionable, and almost cozy.

In Cathedral Square, against the backdrop of the grey and white cathedral, a dozen tourists sit on a dark, curved bench or stand behind it. Some hold the blue, red, and white New Zealand flag while a photographer snaps the group's picture. Nearby, a red-billed gull adds another touch of grey and white when it perches atop an immense statue of Robert Godley, recognized as the founder of Canterbury. The gull catches the tourists' and my attention and provides us with a shared smile.

Vilis, Jānis, and I wind our way to the Christchurch Botanic Gardens, where weeping willows drape the Avon River's banks and mallards swim amid broken shimmers of light beneath the willow curtains. "It's so *liquid,*" Vilis whispers as he gazes intently at the water. Then he catches himself. "Well, I guess it *is* liquid."

Cast-off leaves of non-native horse chestnuts, oaks, and maples layer orange-brown carpets beneath dark, bare limbs. My spirit soars and aches at the familiar sight.

"This feels like fall," Vilis says, breathing in deeply. "I am so much looking forward to winter – Canadian winter, that is. I have so much missed the snow."

Ahead of us, teenagers laugh and shuffle in the leaves, their footsteps a joyous autumn dance. One teen and then another breaks free of the knot, makes a mad dash and leaps into the air, hand outstretched to catch a falling leaf.

May 7

AFTER TEA I ask Vilis, "So, what kind of possum data are you analyzing? I know there are lots of projects. Which one is this data from?"

My husband's eyes dance. "From Tūtaki." That's the valley in the north-central South Island to which my family travelled in September. The boys and I hiked and birded while Vilis helped Landcare technicians dismantle radio telemetry towers.

"Ah. What are the results?" I ask.

"Do you remember what the project was?"

I envision the rain-washed, valley-bottom pastures and steep hills. "I remember some of it. They trapped possums out from an area – was it the forest next to the pastures, or did it include the pastures, too? Then they tested to see if other possums moved into that area."

"They removed possums from the forest right next to the pastures, but there was more to it than that. Farmers often hire contractors to get rid of possums."

"By hunting?" Jānis asks.

Dainis shakes his head. "Naw."

"Probably by trapping or poisoning," Vilis suggests. "After the contractor's finished, someone else checks to see if they did the work before the contractor gets paid. But, if the person checking found there were still possums, some of the contractors were saying that possums moved in from surrounding areas after they had removed all the possums. So, the aim of the study was to see if that's true."

"And is it?" I ask.

My husband laughs. "No. The possums went the other way!"

"They did?" I wasn't expecting that. "Why would they do that?"

Vilis shakes his head. "I don't know. The suggestion is that the disturbance next door scared them off."

I smile. "So, some of the contractors *weren't* doing a good job."

"No, they weren't."

Intriguing.

May 8

AFTER THE boys complete their schooling, I place packs, sleeping bags, tent, storage containers, camp stove, maps, and extra clothes on the floor against a dining room wall. I gather food, towels, and camera equipment and chivvy the boys into adding their personal camping gear to the growing pile. The West Coast beckons, and with two days of fine weather in the forecast, we're off tomorrow to explore it. Punakaiki and its Pancake Rocks. Pororari River and Bullock and Cave Creeks. Truman Track and Fox River Cave. These sites, about 300 kilometres northwest of Lincoln, will offer only a taste of the West Coast, but it'll be a taste rich with *nīkau* palms and tangy with the salt of the Tasman Sea.

May 9

THE SKY is grey, the highway damp, and Dainis's wet socks are drying on the Bomb's dashboard as we drive through West Melton en route to the West Coast. Fallen grape leaves in the vineyard near Andrea and Andy's house blanket the ground with yellow.

"Ah, it's brighter here," Vilis says.

Dainis glances up from the final health exam he's writing while Jānis reviews skin and teeth. "You mean it's a little less grey."

Cloud rises from brown-green hills like steam from the vents and fumaroles of Rotorua and Craters of the Moon. Gone is the parched look of the landscape. In the distance, sunlit cloud pierced by mountain peaks shimmers, beckoning like a magical kingdom. Farther west, long tawny slopes and reaching plateaus remind me of Otago's rangeland and the Lindis Pass area we drove through in late November and early December.

Beyond Porter's Pass, Castle Hill Conservation Area's jumbled limestone formations are like a giant's playground. Unable to resist the lure of the boulders, we pull into a parking area, step onto a "Stile of New Zealand" that Vilis photographs, and cross a page wire fence into fantasy land. Tors (rocky peaks) jut against the sky, their weathered limestone outcrops resembling mobs of misshapen trolls frozen in place by the light. Others lie fractured and broken, collapsed into sprawling mounds of rubble.

Redpolls flit through rock clefts and sweep around towers of stone. Rabbits bound across the boulder-strewn landscape. Roses' red hips and yellow leaves paint bright colours against pale, lichen-wrapped rock. We climb smooth limestone boulders pocked with large holes, and stand against the sky. I spot a New Zealand falcon with prey in its talons and hear the echoes of magpies' songs bounce between rocks. We scramble down from atop gigantic boulders, squeeze through narrow crevices between stone behemoths, and work our way up onto others. Like Ōhinetonga Lagoon on North Island, this is a place out of time, a place caught in wonder. Loathe to leave it, we nonetheless step away from the boulders, cross the stile, and pile into the station wagon.

CASTLE HILL CONSERVATION AREA

Westward, beech forests cloak the slopes at Craigieburn, and Flock Hill resembles a gigantic slip, its side scored by deep rents. Lake Pearson's grey sheet broods between olive and ochre slopes, and distant blue tendrils thread through Waimakariri River's massive bed of grey shingle. The burn that closed the trans-island highway in late March left a trail of fire-scorched slopes and shrub skeletons with blackened, reaching fingers. Past Klondike Corner, half way to our destination, high, beech-covered hills edge the highway. "This is where Jānis and I went camping when you and Dainis were on that Scout camp," Vilis tells me.

I envision the Blue Bomb parked at the base of a hill while my husband and younger son backpack their way up the slope through dense bush.

In the highest reaches of Arthur's Pass, the valley narrows into Ōtira Gorge between steep-sided, bulging mountains scarred by avalanches. Highway, railway, and electricity transmission towers share the narrow corridor, then the railway disappears into 8.5-kilometre Ōtira Tunnel that offers trains safe passage through the spine of the Southern Alps.[30] Here, the highway is pasted to the mountainside, supported by concrete braces and protected from avalanches by concrete shelters. Farther on, it's suspended above ground on a pillared viaduct.

Beyond Ōtira and Aickens, the northbound highway curves southwest and parallels Taramakau River. We cross the river and drive north to Rotomanu, where dairy herds and *pūkeko* amble through lush green pastures. The landscape is noticeably more verdant than in Canterbury. We push on to Stillwater and south to Greymouth on the coast, then north on the coastal highway to Punakaiki and Paparoa National Park. Lumpy hills covered with needle-leaved podocarps flank the road. At Punakaiki, massive limestone cliffs tower over dense coastal rainforest frilled with the flaring leaves of *nīkau* palms and fronds of tree ferns.

A few kilometres north of Punakaiki, amid shrubs and trees sculpted by blasting winds off the Tasman Sea, we turn inland onto Bullock Creek Road. The narrow gravel road parallels dry Bullock Creek, which lies at the base of steep cliffs to both north and south and is posted with warnings of floods after heavy rain. At 5:00 p.m. and with no sign of the Bullock Creek "campground" we were looking for, we set up camp on a patch of grass next to a locked gate. Dainis cooks chilli for supper while Vilis and Jānis erect the tent, after which I place foam mattresses and sleeping bags in our shelter.

PUNAKAIKI RAINFOREST

At dusk, mist gathers like soldiers of a silent army and advances eerily until we're surrounded – our tent coated with their cold white breaths. Vilis reads from C. S. Lewis's *The Voyage of the Dawn Treader*, wherein Eustace creeps into a dead dragon's cave and finds a bracelet that he slips onto his arm before falling asleep, only to wake and find that he himself has become a dragon. "It's different being read to in a tent by candlelight," Jānis says, his eyes lit with the magic of Eustace's adventure blending with our own. "It makes it seem that this could happen."

Beyond our tent and the mist, stars shine like blurry beacons. The forest is alive with wild kiwi cries and moreporks' begging requests. This avian night music is so different from the night's silence at Lake Daniell, where beguilingly beautiful reflections of hills in the lake were belied by the presence of egg-eating mammals – possums in trees beside the hut, and rats scurrying about in the grass in front of the building and chewing on its walls.

In the thickness of this mist-shrouded night, we hear the approaching roar of a vehicle. It halts at the locked gate. The engine quits. A door opens and slams. In the mist, we see nothing and hear no human voice. A short time later, the door opens and slams again. Then we and our unknown neighbour are cloaked in white darkness.

May 10

THIS MORNING, tree silhouettes create black lace against white ground mist. The meadow beside our camp sparkles with dew drops that adorn every grass stem bent beneath its beauty. The Department of Conservation visitor pamphlet for Paparoa National Park states, "Be prepared for rain at any time of the year,"[31] but today, sunshine reigns.

We battle chilly air with a breakfast of steaming porridge sweetened with brown sugar and raisins, and with mugs of hot chocolate. Then, while mist rises against the hills and bearded forests, we walk past a white UV parked next to the gate (its driver asleep in his seat), climb over the barricade, and follow a pasture trail to where a river disappears.

Riddled with caves and sinkholes, the limestone karst landscape of Paparoa National Park creates waterways that are a medley of aboveground passage and belowground entrapment. Bullock Creek is one such trapped river. Soon we encounter one door to its prison – a dry, gravely creek bed with nothing much to see except that past a shallow pool the creek is gone. We listen carefully and hear the trickle of water pouring down into a sinkhole that drains the creek and sends its water into an underground riverbed.[32]

"Is this all?" the boys ask, unimpressed.

"Later, we'll hike to Cave Creek, where the water comes out

again," I tell them.

ON MOUNT BOVIS TRACK

We leave the creek bed and tramp a section of Mount Bovis Track through pastures on a valley floor bounded by tree-clad ridges. We spot goldfinches, shelducks, and plovers, as well as a fantail frolicking in a patch of shrubs. The sound of a pickup truck startles us, and a few minutes later we watch a man attend beehives seemingly in the middle of nowhere. The honey man's movements are quick and efficient. He takes no notice of us or the bees crawling in his hair.

IN LATE morning, we retrace our path to where Mount Bovis Track, one of a web of tracks in the valley, links up with Cave Creek Track. At the base of a plaque beside the path to Cave Creek, a withered bouquet rests on grass, the flowers' brown stems encircled by a yellow ribbon tied into a bow. The plaque itself stands like a sentry too slim and straight for the commemoration it bears — that of fourteen people who lost their lives when an observation platform collapsed on April 28, 1995, sending them plummeting to their deaths on the rocks of the creek bed below. Here, in bright autumn sunshine, we walk toward what was a scene of disaster six years and twelve days ago.

Amid posted warnings of danger, we approach the steeply-cut gorge of Cave Creek near Cave Creek Cave. Downstream from here, the trapped waters of Bullock Creek return to the surface as springs that feed this creek. In times of heavy rainfall, when the underground system of conduits and caves fed by Bullock Creek is filled to capacity, excess water gushes out of Cave Creek Cave into this creek bed and also surges down the normally dry creek bed beside Bullock Creek Road.

In the rich dimness of the gorge below us, mosses and liverworts create lush, velvet tapestries that cover huge rock plates jumbled into heaps in the creek bed, which is dry now, but everywhere speaks of moisture. Cautiously, as though entering a muted, mossy shrine, we descend steep steps to the creek bed and are enveloped by its cool, damp breath. Every rock surface on the gorge walls is green with plant life, as are most of the rounded stones and plates of rock beneath our feet. Fronds of ferns and tree ferns flare outward from the gorge walls, and trees extend crooked limbs that drip long moss tendrils.

While Vilis sets up his camera and tripod to photograph the rich vegetation and brooding creek bed, the boys and I make our way upstream to where a massive, plant-hung wall, split by a narrow crack, looms over us. It marks the resurgence cave of the trapped stream. A circular hole in the cleft wall becomes a target through which my sons and I toss stones and calculate our throwing averages. The sounds of stones quickly hitting water tell of our misses, while stones clattering on rock and eventually plopping into water far below tell of our successes. Each of those long, clattering falls elicits a grin. That a river flows deep beneath this shrouded cave and creek bed is an exciting thought. On the heels of this knee-jerk excitement comes the eerie knowledge that the trapped river sometimes spurts out of the cave and pours through this gorge as a raging torrent.

AT CAVE CREEK CAVE

A dusky New Zealand robin keeps the boys and me company while we toss stones. Later, it lands at the base of a tripod leg while Vilis photographs the creek bed and its lush plant life. We feel the presence of no ghosts, but later find where the old viewing platform must have been – suspended over a sheer drop of at least thirty metres, nearer to the cave entrance than the present stairs. No wonder so many died when the platform collapsed.

I tell Vilis and the boys, "Gary, the Landcare technician, said that a DOC worker he knows had to retrieve the body of his boss, and that he thought some of the victims were Scouts on an outing."

"*Scouts?*" Dainis murmurs in shock. His shoulders slump with grief. (But the technician was wrong about Scouts. Thirteen of the fourteen victims of the Cave Creek Disaster were outdoor recreation students from Tai Poutini Polytechnic in Greymouth. The fourteenth victim, as the tech said, was a Department of Conservation field officer.)[33]

IN MID-AFTERNOON, we break camp and drive to Punakaiki. There, beneath looming limestone cliffs ribbed with rock strata, topped with *nīkau*, and draped with cascades of shrubs and ferns, we locate Pororari River Track. Its entrance is edged with massive clumps of pale-leaved flax, beyond which palms rise in stately elegance and cabbage trees in kinky crookedness, both throwing their blade-like leaves against the sky.

Once on the track, I feel as though we've truly entered the rainforest realm. Vegetation cloaks every surface – ground, rocks, and trees whose trunks provide habitat for perching lilies, clumps of *kiekie* with their trailing vines, and delicate curtains of filmy ferns. The air is ripe with the scent of living and decaying plants whose fronds and leaves thrust into and hang down onto the track in a wild collage of shapes and textures. From a small opening at the forest edge, we look across brown Pororari River to the opposite shore. A solid forest canopy lanced by soaring tree ferns and *nīkau* climbs the hillside like a plush green bath towel rumpled and casually hung over a slant-backed chair. I want to reach across the water and touch it, to feel its softness.

In late afternoon, we book a tent site in a motor camp at Punakaiki's north end and visit a craft shop posted with large notices that possums are pests. The shop sells possum pelts as well as hats, mittens, insoles, and cushion covers made from possum fur (elsewhere, we've seen possum fur nipple warmers). The boys are captivated by small matchboxes decorated with reprints of paintings of New Zealand birds, each box one of a series of forty-five. We leave the craft shop stocked with more than enough matches to last the remainder of our time in this country. Next, we hand over the exorbitant sum of thirty-two dollars for a can of taco beans, a can of peas and corn, a small box of risotto rice, a box of muesli bars, a small packet of cookies, a bar of soap, and six slices of bacon.

Before our evening meal, we walk Punakaiki's stony shore to its south end near Dolomite Point, then cross the highway and duck into low-roofed Punakaiki Cavern. The sound of dripping water greets our ears when we creep into the cave along a muddy trail posted with trail markers. Crystals and a few small stalactites stud the rock ceiling above us. We look for glow-worms but see none, yet the trail markers lure us deeper and deeper into the cave.

"We'd better go back," Vilis warns. "We've only got one torch and my LCD pinpoint light. I wouldn't want to be stuck in here if the flashlight batteries give out."

Jānis begs to go on, then after a moment's consideration, begs just as fervently to go back.

"You'll have to become a spelunker, Jānis," Vilis tells him.

"What's that?" Jānis asks.

"Someone who explores caves," I say.

"I'll be a spelunker," Dainis quips. "Just give me a big stone and I'll throw it into the pool at that cave, and that's the sound it'll make."

Back at camp, the boys chatter and throw things at each other while they supposedly help to cook supper. In drizzle, we hurriedly wash dishes, then take refuge within the tent. Jānis lights his candle lantern – one of the old, battered DB Draught cans we hung outside our tent on Christmas Eve. Vilis suspends it from the tent ceiling before reading aloud more of Eustace's adventures. In the background, surf pounds against the stony beach, traffic chews up silence on the coastal highway, and whispering rain patters on the tent's exterior while the candle sheds its golden light within.

May 11

THE COASTAL forest enveloping Truman Track, three kilometres north of Punakaiki, is a dripping jungle of vines, tree ferns, *nīkau* palms, weeping *rimu*, and broadleaf trees. When we approach the coast, the forest gives way to thick flax swamps laced with gorse, the dense vegetation forming impenetrable barriers on both sides of the path. Wind and rain blast off the Tasman Sea, causing us to duck beneath our umbrellas to avoid the downpour that plasters sheets of water onto our rain pants and rubber boots. At the end of the track, Jānis and I venture down a set of steps and find a dry cavern eroded out of coastal limestone. "There's a cave down here, and it's dry!" I call up to Vilis and Dainis.

They join us in the cavern, and we all watch as the Tasman Sea slams into rock ledges and boils onto the sand. We hustle down another set of steps onto the beach and rest beneath a dripping overhang, keeping a cautious eye on the incoming waves. The thundering tide reaches too close, so we stay only seconds before returning to the higher cavern. There, a huge spider fights the wind, eating silk from its web that stretches and waves in the storm.

We return to camp and find that the tent has been flattened by the wind, and my sleeping bag is wet. Working together, we move the tent to a more sheltered site and erect it again, after which I hang my bag in the drying room of the motor camp's kitchen and dining complex. Our hair stringy from the rain, we cook grilled cheese sandwiches and hot chocolate for lunch as clouds lift and sunshine streams into the kitchen.

During the afternoon, that sunshine battles dark clouds and drizzle over Punakaiki. For our second exploration of the day, we stride through rainforest and flax swamps toward Pancake Rocks. On one side of the track, a *nīkau* clothed in green ferns wears a cummerbund of leaf bases decorated with sprays of red fruit. On the track's opposite side, supplejack vines create tangled artworks against a backdrop of flamboyant green. I catch glimpses of these as we walk and know that beyond them, like ghosts in the rainforest, are more images of beauty that I can't see.

As we near the coast, we see the Pancake Rocks – eroded towers of limestone sculpted by surf and sea spray. The stacks of thin limestone layers are piled high into pillars and flowerpots and craggy sculptures of dimly recognized creatures. Wild water surges through channels between the rock formations. It slams into solid rock walls and shatters into froth that sprays high in the air, some of it touching our faces. The boys laugh and exclaim over the power of the surf, and when weary of it, lounge in curved rock seats built into protective stone walls.

PANCAKE ROCKS, PUNAKAIKI

Hungry for more of the cluttered rainforest we walked through yesterday, we return to Pororari River Track in late afternoon. The tidal river is shallow and bedded with golden-brown stones. The forest beside it drips rain onto us while we again walk its edge, enjoying New Zealand's version of rainforest – one of the most diverse ecosystems on earth.

LATER, RAIN forces us to cook our evening meal in the camp kitchen. By the time we finish eating, the precipitation is a downpour. "I'm glad we're not at Bullock Creek today," I tell Vilis, envisioning water flooding onto the narrow Bullock Creek Road and blocking access to the coast.

"Speaking of flooding, I'd better check the tent." He returns a short time later. "It was leaking in three or four places, so I moved us into a cabin."

After washing and drying dishes, we share a table with two talkative men from Christchurch. One dark and one fair, the pair recently completed a run around the top of Abel Tasman National Park. The fair man recalls the 1970s when the Kiwi dollar was worth more than the American dollar. "It was worth a dollar fifteen," he says.

"What happened?" I ask.

He shrugs. "Big investments. Big spending. Big loans."

I offer my "No Big Dangerous Carnivores Theory" about why Kiwis are such thrill seekers, adding, "When you go hiking or camping in New Zealand, the only real dangers are weather and difficult terrain."

The fair man tilts his head, a pensive look on his face. "Well," he finally says, "I suppose the only thing that might kill you would be…another camper."

With a jolt, I recall the thick mist at our camp beside Bullock Creek and the eerie sound of an unseen vehicle approaching on a lonely road in the darkness.

Dainis cruises the dining room and collects a new beer cap from a male diner who is sharing avocado salad and cheese soup with a woman. The man wears a hand-knitted wool cap and has eyebrow and ear rings. At another table, a couple playing cards laughs and speaks a language I don't recognize. He's golden-skinned, dark-haired, and wears a nose ring. She's a brown-haired Caucasian. In these couples, the men are more decorated than the women.

May 12

AFTER ANOTHER hot porridge breakfast, we pack our wet tent and soggy belongings into the car and study the sky. Drizzle mists the air. We debate among ourselves and finally decide to tramp Fox River Cave Track and see how that goes.

North of Punakaiki, we locate the track's trailhead just past the bridge over Fox River. Once on the trail, lush rainforest encloses us. At times, the trail is a narrow path that edges around steep slopes, and at others, it's a broad highway beneath a canopy of tree ferns, the path littered with rusty fallen fronds. Small wet rocks roll beneath our feet like ball bearings on one stretch of track. On another, Dainis and Jānis roll their pant legs up onto their thighs to avoid wetting them in icy, fast-flowing water as we wade shallow Fox River.

The entrance to Fox River Cave is a massive gash in a cliff face draped with ferns and other vegetation. We sidle around a huge boulder that partially obstructs the opening.

"Now *this* is a cave!" Jānis declares.

The vaulted ceiling at the entrance drops to near Vilis's head height as we penetrate deeper into the cave, and the passageway shrinks to a narrow corridor with wet, rippled walls. Stalactites and stalagmites stab like rough, pointed teeth into the space around us. Our torch beams flash off calcite formations that look like drinking straws and soft-serve ice cream swirls hanging from the ceiling. Our voices echo in the darkness.

CROSSING FOX RIVER

The track ends 200 metres within the cliff, so we turn and retrace our steps. As we approach the yawning entrance, light shines vivid green through the overhanging plant curtain, beckoning us with the promise of lushness beyond. The boys stand in the entrance, their bodies stark black child shapes against the green light.

We return to Punakaiki and picnic at the visitor centre, where a sturdy-legged, flightless woodhen or *weka* (one of the native birds beautifully portrayed on the boys' matchboxes) scurries around our table. Its lumpy brown body is reminiscent of a kiwi's, although the *weka* has obvious wings. Again we study the sky. Brooding purple clouds hang over the limestone cliffs, and fine sprays of mist drift down on us.

Finally, we take a chance that serious rain will hold off and rent wet suits and four bright blue river kayaks to paddle Pororari River. For two hours, we kayak the brown tidal waterway edged with the rich rainforest we explored twice from land.

KAYAKING PORORARI RIVER

When the broad waterway near the coast gives way to rocky riffles and rapids upriver, I bring up the rear, struggling to fight the water's power while my adventurous husband and sons manoeuvre their boats deftly beyond the eddy in which I find a haven. Enviously,

I watch Vilis lead the boys upstream among the riffles until at last they allow their kayaks to swing with the current, bringing them back to me. Again, as on the day I crashed while mountain biking at Bottle Lake Forest Park, I feel totally inadequate. Although my fears sometimes – like today – get in the way, I yearn to be the strong, adventurous woman who doesn't back away from risks, who doesn't freeze in a tight situation, who can tackle any outdoor adventure. I'm not there yet.

At dusk, we head south from Punakaiki on the first leg of the three-and-a-half-hour drive back to Lincoln. In the darkening sky, what look like long-winged bats blast landward. With a start, I realize the dozen flying creatures aren't bats at all. They're seabirds called Westland petrels. I add yet one more "lifer" to my New Zealand bird list as we drive past the petrels' breeding grounds.

WESTLAND PETRELS

Agile in air and on water, soot-coloured Westland petrels fly landward from the Tasman Sea at dusk and crash-land in rainforests near Punakaiki to lay and incubate eggs and tend nestlings in burrows in the forest soil. Unlike other petrel species that once nested on New Zealand's main islands, Westland petrels are big and aggressive enough to make introduced predators think twice about raiding their nests for eggs or young. They have a fighting chance for survival so long as their only remaining strip of nesting habitat near Punakaiki is protected from encroaching forestry, mining, and farming. These industries have already shrunk the breeding territory of the remaining 20 000 petrels to an eight-kilometre strip of forested hills.[34]

South of Greymouth, we turn east toward Arthur's Pass. Above us, the moon is a pregnant woman strolling in the night, her belly huge and rounded, wisps of dream clouds about her, the stars her companions. She is Luna.

The boys are asleep in the back seat. Jānis crashed soon after supper, exhausted from our day of tramping and paddling. Dainis nodded off later, after he tired of blitzing falling aliens on the palm computer. Vilis dodges possums – dead and alive. Unable to miss a dead one, he winces when the car's tires thud into the solid lump. "At least it wasn't hard, like a rock," he mutters. "At least it had some give."

It's a lonely road. We've passed only two other vehicles, both motor homes, in the east-bound lane and perhaps a dozen and a half vehicles travelling west. Finally, the mountains are behind us. Darkness streams past as the Bomb makes her run for Lincoln, with Luna by her side.

May 13

AFTER CHURCH, Nancy Borrie's shoulders droop. I just told her that our return flight to Canada is booked for June 23rd. "That's the problem with living in a place like Lincoln," she says, "where people like you come and go, staying for only a short time. It's hard to form relationships, knowing that you'll never see those people again after they leave – at least not in this world."

I am truly blind. I never thought of that. During our time in this country, I focused on my family's periodic feelings of loneliness and isolation, on how we needed to make contacts and friends. I didn't consider how hard it must be to reach out again and again to form friendships with newcomers you know will leave the country in a few months or years.

"But God gives us strength," Nancy continues stoically, "and I've learned to think of each of those relationships as another bright thread in the tapestry of life."

DURING THE afternoon, my family is again drawn to Christchurch

Botanic Gardens, today alive with families lured outdoors by warm sunshine. Brightly clad toddlers toddle among trees and along paths. Older children race across lawns and drop from low tree branches to the ground. Beneath the huge, spreading limbs of the fern-leaved beech, a wee girl is a piece of magic at play. Dressed in pale pink overalls, she scoops up armfuls of amber leaves and flings them into the air. Beneath a straw hat decorated with a green rose, her strawberry blond ringlets bob and dance as she toddles forward and kicks a pile of leaves with her dark pink wellies. Her excited cry is laughter at its sweetest. Passers-by stop to watch her, but she has eyes only for the leaves and for a dark-haired man with arms outstretched.

At the edge of a pond across the parking lot from the gardens, a wee boy sidles closer and closer to the water while he tosses bread to ducks – his mother periodically tugging him back. Nearby, other children crowd around a man piloting a remote-control sailboat cruising among the ducks, its white sail bright against dark water.

'Isn't it *good* to feel the sun today?' Nancy asked this morning, before hastily adding, 'I'm not complaining about the rain. I know we've needed it, but I just felt that if only I could have a *little* bit of sun today…'

It's here, drying the earth and warming our hands and souls.

May 15

THIS MORNING, fallen leaves are wild creatures racing before the wind. Clouds billow and churn with an ominous greyness, pouring over the Port Hills like a beast in search of prey. A cold white Antarctic lion prowls to the south of this country, shaking the land with its roaring breath and lunging at it with icy claws. When I drive home from the rink, the lion's frigid breath whips drizzle, then rain and hail onto the car's windshield.

The rink was cooler today. Some of the Coffee Club skaters shivered and said they don't enjoy skating as much when the venue is so cold. Yet, the Alpine Ice Sports Centre is balmy in comparison with the unheated rink in our Nova Scotia village of Tatamagouche, where toes, ears, and fingers often feel the stinging, numbing grip of winter temperatures that plunge far below the freezing point.

IN LATE afternoon, Vilis asks with a smile, "So, what's going on? I come home and hear this wild group of kids outside."

"They're playing hide and seek," I answer distractedly, immersed in labelling photographic slides. "Ben and Elizabeth Peters came over." The lion's breath still lingers, cold and blustery, although this morning's barrage of hail and rain was brief. The sky cleared in early afternoon and lured our sons and their friends from across the street to play outdoors.

When dusk falls, I drive Dainis and Ben to the tennis courts in Springston, five kilometres west of Lincoln, for their winter tennis lesson. Yet my mind is elsewhere, skimming North Island and reliving images of rainforests and volcanic and geothermal landforms. This small country possesses a mind-boggling diversity of landscapes, many of which we've had the privilege of exploring. And we're not done yet. When fine weather returns to Westland, we'll make a final run through Arthur's Pass to the West Coast and south to the Fox and Franz Josef Glaciers. We need that ice-coloured thread for *our* New Zealand tapestry. We'll tuck it in among the lush greens and tawny browns, the raw reds, stony greys, and luminous sea-greens.

In Springston, lights high above the tennis courts are brilliant white beacons in the night. While a beginner class finishes its lesson, Dainis stands by the fence with his arms close to his sides and his hands in his pockets. "It'll be good to do the warm-up," he tells Ben, "because then we'll warm up!"

May 17

FEEL THE *ice. Feel the edges. Feel the weight transfer.* The journey toward backward cross-cuts is like the Godley Head tunnel we explored in September – dark, with peep holes along the way. I've passed a few of the peep holes. I can now scull or pump my way around the rink. I can push myself backward with mini-strokes, lifting my feet from the ice. Suddenly, the tunnel curves, its walls brightened by an unexpected peep hole. Unconsciously, I'm pumping backward and lifting my feet as though to position each for a cross-cut.

When dance music comes on, I tackle the Dutch Waltz with moderate success, but lose the timing altogether for the Canasta Tango. Then Danielle is at my side, guiding me through the quick, four-beat steps. At the tango's finish, we hear a resounding thud on the ice behind us and turn to see a woman lying motionless on her side. I recognize her as another new face, another D name – Dora. Knees bent, hands halfway to her face, she's motionless.

"She's gone and knocked herself out, I think," Danielle murmurs.

Already, skaters cluster around the fallen woman, and an ice pack is on the way. Slowly, almost imperceptibly, she begins to move. Then she slowly sits up and is helped from the ice. Dizzy and with a huge lump on the back of her head, she's checked out by Daphne and watched over by two new Coffee Club skaters whose names I don't know. Later, after hot chocolate in Zamboni's, Delia offers to drive Dora and her bicycle home.

There's kindness in this cool place. And compassion. Despite having no bond other than a desire to skate and a no-strings-attached membership in Coffee Club, this group of casual skaters has become a whole far greater than the sum of its parts.

MY SONS and the preacher's kids from across the street – Josh, who's Dainis's age, Ben, who's a couple years younger, Sam, who's Jānis's age, and little Elizabeth, who's about five years old – have become almost inseparable. Today after school, Dainis and Jānis cycle with Josh and Ben on their paper route, then play hide and seek in our yard with the all the Peters children. The dark strokes of those early months of loneliness in a foreign country are being erased by as much play and companionship as possible.

May 19

SALT. I measure a teaspoonful and add it to the batter for another baked-peach breakfast even as I hear on the radio that 60 000 tonnes of salt are harvested annually from South Island's evaporation ponds at Lake Grassmere near Blenheim. I remember the flat country there and the salt works sign. What I wasn't aware of when we drove to North Island is that, as I learn this morning, the harvest of Grassmere salt during a six-week season beginning in March yields enough (up to 6 000 tonnes per day) to supply all of New Zealand with table salt and the meat and hide industries with a good portion of what they require as well.

After Vilis and Jānis return from the rink, Vilis tells me, "I want to go somewhere where we can walk and walk and see all around."

"The Port Hills?" I guess.

"Exactly."

The four of us pack food and tramping supplies and pile into the Bomb, taking young Sam Peters with us for the outing. We drive the now-familiar route from Lincoln east past Tai Tapu to Gebbies Pass on the crater rim of Banks Peninsula's Lyttelton Volcano, and then descend to the south shore of Lyttelton Harbour. The twisting shoreline road leads us east to Orton Bradley Park, which technically isn't in the Port Hills, but has the same feel – big tawny hills that provide grazing for countless sheep. In the park, we choose Tableland Route for our hike.

ON TABLELAND ROUTE IN ORTON BRADLEY PARK

Autumn sunshine pours down as my family and Sam follow a

track uphill through open grazing land. After checking a cattle pasture for bulls, we walk through a herd of lowing cows before climbing a stile to cross a tall fence. Beyond the fence, the track leads into a gum tree plantation, where the menthol smell of eucalyptus permeates the air. Long, pointed leaves litter the track with brown lance tips, and empty fallen seed capsules look like clusters of miniature bronze goblets. As we pause for a rest, Sam pants, "You have to pace yourself. If you sprint at the start, you'll be all puffed before you reach the top!"

Past the eucalypt plantation, the track climbs gently and follows the sides of grazed slopes sweeping up to Kaituna Pass and Mount Bradley. We stop for a rest and look behind us. Huge pine branches fan out against the glistening silver backdrop of Lyttelton Harbour. Sheep inspect us with raised heads. Half a year ago, we grew frustrated at sharing our tramps with sheep; now, surprisingly, it's good to see them again. The boys exclaim over a ewe with fleece so heavy we wonder if she escaped shearing, and over her lamb with a long, undocked tail.

As a trio, Dainis, Jānis, and Sam romp ahead of Vilis and me or lag behind on uphill stretches. They chatter, snigger, and call out with laughter in their voices. Their pockets are filled with the dried peas that Jānis and Dainis gathered from the pea field behind North Belt after Crop & Food Research had finished combining. The boys position the peas in slingshots and blast them into cow patties and at trees or the poles marking the track.

On the return half of the three-kilometre loop track, we hike a wooded side trail – Waterfall Track – that climbs beside Wharau Stream. The path provides river rocks and pools as new targets for the boys' marksmanship. When we pass a yellow poison bait dispenser in a tree alongside the trail, the temptation is irresistible. All three boys draw back their slingshot elastics and let go with a yell and a shot. Jānis's pea thwacks into the dispenser's open mouth and knocks out a bright green cylinder of poisoned bait intended for possums. The pellet lies conspicuously foreign among the browns and dark greens of the shaded forest floor, its neon colour a warning to foraging birds.

"Are you sure this is the way back?" Sam asks after we rejoin the loop track.

"We're going back a different way than we came," Vilis explains, "so we can see different things."

"It's a loop," I add, and our reassurances seem to mollify Sam.

In the valley bottom, we tramp through sheep paddocks alongside the stream. Near a green-painted stile, a weathered information plaque catches my eye. "There was a flax mill here," I call out to Vilis and the boys. "It says that Adam Chalmer established a flax mill on this site in 1870, and that it was used until the 1890s, when steamships were introduced."

All that remains of the mill is a huge flat stone with a hole that's roughly square in shape cut into its centre. The stone gives no hint of what its purpose was. In fact, there's little to give us any sense of a bustling mill. However, according to the information plaque, flax leaves collected on the hillsides were mechanically beaten (using the stone, I assume) to separate the strong fibres from the surrounding tissues. Afterward, the fibres were washed and dried before a second beating. Then they were baled into bundles and shipped from Lyttelton. This mill, then, was part of the flax fibre and rope export industry (1840s to 1890s, according to the plaque) that kept New Zealand on the map of international trading when sealing and whaling industries began to fade.

On the drive home, the three boys chatter up a storm in the back seat. With Sam as a focus for their attention, Dainis and Jānis haven't been arguing or asking innumerable and sometimes unanswerable questions. This has relieved Vilis and me of our roles as referees and encyclopaedias. The sudden time and space my husband and I have to ourselves is so unusual it's unfamiliar, even uncomfortable. As we discuss banal topics and disagree about taking photographs, I realize how much of my focus has been on my children during this time in New Zealand.

Again, we stop for ice cream treats. This time it's Hokey Pokey for me, Cookies and Cream for Jānis and Vilis, and Goody, Goody Gumdrops (again!) for Dainis. Sam chooses Passion Fruit, then hesitates before his first lick to ask if we are really buying this ice cream for him.

Vilis assures him, "It's yours, Sam."

More laughter – *buddy* laughter – fills the back seat on the return drive to Lincoln.

May 22

BEYOND THE bedroom curtains, I hear the scrape of windshield wipers across a windshield and know the road verges will be white with frost when I drive to the rink. I scramble out of bed and run to the dining room to plug in an electric heater, then race back to the bedroom and dress, all the while shivering.

To warm the house, I collect kindling and firewood from the garage and light a fire in the small pot-bellied stove. I wonder if Jim – the farmer whose son, Jason, is in Cubs – knew a cold snap was coming when he offered us some firewood. More likely, he knew from long experience how unpredictable New Zealand weather is and how poorly insulated Kiwi houses are. "They only heat them as much as they have to," a Canadian expat told Vilis and me after a recent church service.

Muffins. We need muffins. While stirring walnuts and peaches into batter, I hear a radio report that tells of an early winter storm blasting Otago, Southland, and Fiordland. Police are urging drivers to stay off Otago's icy, snow-covered roads, and drivers headed from Te Ānau to Milford are warned that chains are essential. The white lion's breath blasts out of the south again. His forepaws are braced on Southland and Fiordland while his mane shakes snow and ice onto Otago.

DURING THE evening, Lincoln Scout Hall is lively with International Night at Cubs. Already, a boy with Scottish ancestry has shown his kilt, and already, my family has led the Cubs in singing the Canadian canoeing song *Land of the Silver Birch.* Dainis also displayed the Canadian flag his 1st Tatamagouche Scout Troop leader sent the Lincoln troop in March and read aloud her accompanying letter describing winter camping in Nova Scotia. Now, Ruchika Tandon, a young Indian girl who lives in the house behind ours, hands out a traditional Indian sweet called *barfi,* which she says is usually made for special occasions like weddings. The first Cub to which she offers the sweet shrinks away, but he hastily asks for a piece after the second Cub in line pronounces it delicious with a loud, "Yum!"

"It tasted like a cross between toffee and butter candies," Jānis tells Vilis and me after the meeting ends, before he races off to romp with other Cubs.

A visiting Cub leader asks Vilis's and my permission to invite Jānis and Dainis to give a presentation about Canada to her pack in Christchurch. While we talk, I glance beyond her to a window. Through it, I see flakes of snow caught in the bright light of a street lamp. Winter has arrived in Lincoln.

May 23

THIS MORNING, the radio reports that for the first time in recorded history, snow lies on the ground in Ōkārito (There's none in Lincoln, despite the flakes that fell last night.). Halfway up South Island's West Coast, Ōkārito typically experiences winter weather ameliorated by the warming influence of the Tasman Sea – that being the reason this snowfall is so unusual. The town lends its name to a lagoon that's a sanctuary for the white heron, sacred to the Māori – the *kōtuku* – and is, along with the Fox and Franz Josef Glaciers, one of our final destinations in this country.

Restless, I listen intently to weather and road reports, on edge with indecision regarding our planned drive to the West Coast tomorrow. The cold snap, which descended on South Island three weeks earlier than usual, hangs over our plans like a dark warrior brandishing an ice-edged sword. I phone the visitor's centre in Arthur's Pass Village and listen to a recorded message that advises chains are essential (we have none) and more snow is on the way.

We'll bide our time. Perhaps the warrior will retreat.

May 24

VILIS MURMURS sleepily, "Shouldn't you have been up at six to write? That's forty-five minutes ago."

I shiver. "I was too cold." All night, even beneath our goose-down duvet, I felt the frigid touch of the cold snap.

"Does this mean I won't hear from the kitchen, 'Vili, it's time to get up. The fire's going.'?"

"Not today. It's your turn to light the fire. I was cold all night."

"But, I don't know if I *can*."

"You always did back home."

"But this is *New Zealand*."

"New Zealand men are macho."

My husband snorts with laughter. "But about this? I mean, I can see jumping off a cliff tied to a rope, but *this*?" We guffaw, and he leaps out of bed and into his clothes, drawing in sharp, sucking breaths against the cold.

AT THE rink in mid-morning, Kim Lewis puts on a CD of fast instrumental classics. Alex, a new Coffee Club skater in her twenties, nods her head in approval. The music makes me want to move, to skate fast, to try things I've never done before. In this place, I reach for the cold, for the ice, and will my blades to really feel it while I practice sculling, pumping, stroking, as well as inside and outside edges around a circle. Then I tackle backward crosscuts. Danielle takes my fingers, guiding me. When she releases my fingertips, the speed is frightening. My heart beats wildly as I push backwards, carefully cross over, and then execute one crosscut after another.

May 25

I RUN my gaze over Lyttelton Harbour and the Port Hills on Banks Peninsula. "These cattle and sheep have one of the finest views I've ever known," I tell Dainis.

He laughs. "Do you suppose they're smart enough to appreciate it?"

"You never know." Exhaustion floats about me like a woolly, weighted cloud as we pass The Tors – massive, vertical outcrops of volcanic rock that jut from the Port Hills' skyline near Christchurch. Yet I was the one who railed against spending a sunlit afternoon indoors and who suggested we explore more of Crater Rim Walkway.

STILE AND VIEW FROM CRATER RIM WALKWAY NEAR THE TORS

"I'm so much enjoying this," Vilis says repeatedly while he photographs the harbour, the cows against the backdrop of the harbour, and on the hilltops, the rough, knobby volcanic rock upon which we walk.

Jānis races across a stretch of old lava. "I like this kind of rock. It looks like it should be slippery, but it's not. It has good grip."

It has amazing grip. We cling to knobby protrusions and scramble up onto a rocky headland that overlooks Lyttelton, its dockyards, and Bridle Path – the track by which Canterbury settlers crossed the hills from Lyttelton to Christchurch a century and a half ago. Now it's a groomed road.

After we scramble down from our vantage point, we rejoin Crater Rim Walkway, and then abandon it to circle in front of The Tors. Tussocks of grass invite us to sit and rest among them, and we gaze out over Christchurch, spotting a cluster of downtown skyscrapers, Hagley Park, Jade Stadium, and what we think is the roof of the Alpine Ice Sports Centre. In the distance, purple clouds spew precipitation onto the foothills of the Southern Alps. Above us, clouds cast chilling shadows, the sun a refugee among them. A southwest wind – the breath of the white lion – nips our hands and faces with its sharp teeth.

DAINIS AND JĀNIS IN TUSSOCK GRASSLAND NEAR THE TORS

May 27

THERE'S A wildness in the sky; there's a wildness upon the earth. Rain and hail pelt the house and yard, slamming down their harsh, staccato message of power, of challenge. In the yard, young warriors respond, their voices lifted in wild cries, their wet hair plastered against their heads. The power of the sky is in their limbs as they run, the challenge of the dark clouds in their arms as they vault over the low board fence. There's no safety for the enemies' guarded flag, and again and again it's captured, only to be returned.

Darkness falls.

Vilis calls the warriors – Josh and Sam, Sachin (Ruchika's brother), Dainis, and Jānis – into the house for hot chocolate. When they finish their drinks, I suggest they stay in and dry off.

"No way!" Dainis tells me. "It's great out there."

"It's *awesome* out there!" Josh adds.

The warriors rush outside, their wild cries lifting to the fearsome sky.

May 28

MY BREATH is a white cloud in the dining room, the supremely wicked laptop, a cold weight on my thighs as I write. I rise from my chair to add more wood to the fire, kneeling like a supplicant and raising my hands toward the stove's warmth. With the outdoor temperature only a few degrees above freezing, and with cold rain bursting down on Lincoln, the little stove is a weak defence against icy dampness that invades the bungalow. Winter's sudden onset has enveloped my family in the same bone-chilling cold we experienced at North Belt in late August. Kiwis, with their lack of central heating, are one tough bunch of people.

WITH OUR time in this country growing short, my sons have completed most of their academic requirements for the year, allowing us to tidy up loose ends. As in August and September, recent days of cold rain and wild winds have limited our outdoor excursions, so we've had plenty of time to focus on this task. And there's a huge difference in the atmosphere in our "school," compared with those early months – the boys' initial loneliness is long gone. Now, my family awaits a forecast of clear weather through the Southern Alps for a final multi-day adventure. The glaciers are calling.

June 1

BENEATH A brilliant sun, fallen leaves lay in golden carpets beside
Gerald Street. Ice on the far end of the Lincoln University tennis
courts gleams in the shade of a hedge beyond the fence. When I
remove my jacket and later the sweatpants covering my shorts, the
other female tennis players rib me about wearing summer clothes in
winter.

"How hot does it get in – where is it? Nova Scotia?" tennis
coach Chris asks.

"The hottest would be in the low thirties," I answer, meaning
the Celsius temperature scale.

She tilts her head, dark sunglasses hiding her eyes. "And
what's the coldest it gets?"

"The low thirties – in the opposite direction."

The women laugh and shiver.

LATER, WHILE my family eats tea, I ask Vilis, "Any letters?" I'm
craving news from home.

"No."

"Any e-mail letters?"

"Not really." His eyes fill with mischief. "Just something sent
on to me by Andrea from someone asking if Mr. Nams will have his
deliverables ready by the thirtieth of June, and if not, then why not
and what does he intend to do about it?"

Confused, I ask, "Deliverables? What are they?"

"As part of getting this fellowship from Landcare Research, I
wrote up something saying that I would have a paper ready to submit

to a refereed journal based on my research done in Tongariro Forest. That would be the deliverables."

"But you don't have a paper," I say slowly.

"No," he admits.

I study my husband. "So-o, did you tell him no and why not?"

"Well, yes and no." Vilis laughs in some embarrassment. "I wrote a response that was only intended for Andrea, but she sent it on to him."

I feel my eyes widen. "What did it say?"

"Well, it said no, I didn't have the deliverables ready, and they would definitely not be done on time because there weren't enough animals. As for what could be done about it, I gave five options: (1) introduce stoats to Tongariro Forest, (2) make up fake data, (3) do some modeling, (4) use the EAHW test – the Eyeball And Hand Waving test, where you look at the area, wave your hands, and say, 'I think what's going on is...' and (5) write up a paper anyways, just to have a good time reading the reviewers' comments."

With some trepidation, I ask, "And what did he say?"

"Well, he wrote back saying that another option would be to shoot the person who wrote the objective for me!"

"Really?" Relief floods through me. "It's a good thing he's got a sense of humour. Another sort of person could have been quite...*nasty* about it."

Vilis nods, his smile wry. "Yes."

June 2

THIS MORNING, black swans and whitecaps decorate Lake Ellesmere's wind-whipped water. Sunlight flashes gold onto Banks Peninsula's rugged hills. Dense clumps of pampas grass growing alongside the Christchurch–Akaroa highway fly shaggy white seed heads like a thousand wind socks warning of wild weather. Near Birdlings Flat, the road turns inland, sweeps past the agitated grey of Lake Forsyth, then twists and climbs to Montgomery Park Scenic Reserve, our tramping destination for the day.

The track (part of the Port Levy to Hilltop Summit Walkway) immerses us in lush evergreen podocarp forest, the likes of which once covered vast expanses of New Zealand's South Island. A giant *tōtara* dwarfs the boys, its buttressed and fissured trunk variegated with greens and greys of lichens, mosses, and ferns. Massive *matai* display thick trunks hammered with blood-red dents. In the forest understory, tree fuchsias throw twisted, tangled branches to the sky, their papery orange bark hanging in tatters. Jutting rocks force us to clamber onto and over them, and the steep trail is greasy with wet leaves and mud. As we climb, mature forest gives way to regenerating bush that in turn gives way to grassland after we scramble up through a gap between steep-sided bluffs.

Atop an exposed bluff, wind tears at our hair. Snow lies in scattered patches on and near the track. Old *tōtara* trunks and stumps strewn haphazardly over rocky hilltops resemble silver Pickup Sticks. Clouds and sun battle, casting shadow and light onto knife-edged ridges that angle down from Akaroa Volcano's crater rim to Akaroa Harbour.

"Hey! Here's a natural Stile of New Zealand," Jānis calls. He steps over the top strand of a page wire fence, his passage aided by piles of rock on both sides of the barrier. The stile leads only to a bluff's broken crown, so Jānis crouches near the fence, stares at the sweeping landscape, and carefully retraces his steps.

Chilled by the frigid wind, we sink gratefully into dense beds of bracken fern in the lee of a rock outcrop and eat our sandwiches, fruit, and cookies. Then we climb again, with dry grass and rock beneath our feet. Atop a rise, a lone, wind-sheared, half-dead *tōtara* stands like a forgotten sentinel among fallen comrades.

From the summit of Rocky Peak at 700 metres, Banks Peninsula is breathtaking in its beauty. To the north, Pigeon Bay is a shimmering silver tongue. To the southwest, Akaroa Harbour broods beneath billowing clouds. In the northwest, razorback ridges rise to Mount Sinclair's snow-dusted peak. In the east, gentler slopes drop to paddocks and farm buildings in the valley.

IN MONTGOMERY PARK SCENIC RESERVE

Arms outstretched, Dainis grins as he leans back on the fierce wind, his entire weight balanced on his heels. Beyond him, storm clouds pour down into the valley. We take heed, circle behind the lookout, and plunge downward through tangled conspiracies of ferns and shrubs. Bush lawyer clings and tears, leaving blood trickling down Vilis's hands and forearms as he breaks trail. At lower elevations, sheep graze on slopes that are greening up from May rains and drink from a seepage pond caught on a hill's lip.

Our downhill tramp is swift, as it was in Ōkuti Valley Scenic Reserve we explored in early September, which lies beyond a ridge to the south of us now. On reaching the road, we blurt out ice cream flavours with *oohs* and *ahs* of anticipation.

June 3

COOL, STILL air is the touch of night on the brow of day as the sun sets and I walk Lincoln's streets. Seed pods of a *kōwhai* tree growing in a garden hang like flat brown pea pods dried on the stem and hidden by thick clusters of divided leaves of this, New Zealand's national tree. In Liffey Reserve, the introduced English oaks – as stubborn in dropping their leaves as they were in unfurling them – create a mosaic of pale rust on the ground and against the sky. The clear whistles of starlings arrow through chilling air.

I notice our old mailbox is overflowing with fliers. A moment later, in the distance, I see Vilis and our sons crossing North Belt from the access road to the rugby field, where they again launched an experimental rocket, this latest one a sturdy cardboard tube filled with fireworks' gunpowder and ignited by a fuse passing through a hole in a stiff plastic base. If I didn't know them, I'd see them only as a tall man and two boys walking quickly, their voices animated, their words indistinguishable.

A grey and white cat sits atop a high wooden fence, surveying its world. When I stop to speak to it, it jumps down and rubs against my legs. I leave it scratching its back on the footpath and walk to the domain (recreation park), where two boys kick a rugby ball on the emerald field. The tennis courts are grey and bare, completely taken over by netball posts and hoops that open to the sky as though they were cups beseeching an offering. Across North Belt, a camellia wears a sprinkling of layered pink blossoms on its dress of shiny green leaves. Lincoln's walled gardens, with their spring wisteria and summer roses, have drawn inwards, shadowing their hearts.

I return home, where Vilis is splitting wood for the little stove. The boys are hanging out with him.

"Know what happened?" Dainis asks me.

I see controlled excitement in his face. "What happened?"

"The bottom blew off." He pauses, before adding excitedly, "But then the rest of it shot up eighty to a hundred feet!"

"Eighty to a hundred *feet*? Wow!"

"It was the best rocket yet!" Jānis crows. "At first, we couldn't find where it came down. When we went looking for it, we looked back and saw that the bottom part was burning on the ground. It was sending out tons of smoke!"

Finally, a rocket that truly rocketed.

Later, Vilis and I watch Dainis pace about in the dining room, oblivious to us as he relives the rocket launch. He punches the air in victory and exclaims under his breath, "*Yeah! It was great!*"

June 4

AT THE rink, I note Jānis's nervousness. "Are you all right, or do you want me to stay until it's time for your warm-up?"

"Yes, please," he tells me.

The last skater in the Pre-Elementary Ladies event of the Centaurus Ice Club Championships has almost finished her program, and Jānis's event is next.

Moments later, a voice calls his name over the loudspeaker, and he takes to the ice to warm up with several Elementary Ladies. This time, he's the only competitor in his event – Elementary Men. He pushes hard through the six-minute warm-up and looks strong and confident when he skates out to his starting position. Then

Jurassic Park's majestic score rises, propelling him through footwork sequences, spirals, jumps, and whirlpooling him into spins. I see the speed and consistency of his sit-spin and remember how he was falling on his butt with that spin when we arrived in New Zealand. I see the surprising height of his loop jump and recall him muttering earlier in the year, 'The loop is my worst jump.' I watch him head into the entry for his axel and recall Kim Lewis's excitement last week. 'He landed axels!' she shouted. 'I'm having champagne for lunch!' Today, the axel eludes him, but his skate is a good one. The judges agree. For his first open marks ever, they award him 3.2, 3.5, 3.5 for technical merit and 3.0, 3.6, and 3.5 for presentation. We're thrilled.

"Good skate!" I tell Jānis when he joins the rest of us in the stands.

He smiles modestly, his eyes shining.

"Do you get nervous when you skate in a competition?" Vilis asks him.

Jānis considers for a moment, then answers, "Sometimes I'm nervous before I get on the ice, but once I'm on the ice, all I think about is skating."

A short time later, we drive to Lyttelton and tramp up historic Bridle Path, pausing to look down onto the harbour town. The dockyard bustles with the noisy loading of a container ship. Sailboats skim Lyttelton Harbour's blue water. A tugboat guides a red-and-grey container ship to the dockside, and the Black Cat ferry lies in wait for passengers. I try to imagine what the scene looked like a century and a half ago, when a rough path was hurriedly surveyed as the route for Canterbury's new arrivals to make their way from Lyttelton over the Port Hills to the Canterbury Plain. The *Charlotte Jane* arrived only six weeks after surveying began, and the track wasn't finished until a month after that.[35]

"What a beautiful day!" Vilis sighs. "It's hard to believe that only six days ago that cold wind was blasting us on those hilltops." He's referring to Montgomery Park Scenic Reserve.

"*Six* days?" inquires Dainis.

"That wasn't six days ago," I comment. "It was yesterday."

"*Saturday*," Dainis corrects us both.

Two days ago. "Really?" Vilis looks mystified. "Is that only how long ago it was?"

His confusion is understandable. We've crammed so many jaunts and activities into our time here in New Zealand that the essence of one experience soon slips away and is replaced by new experiences layered one on top of the other. Perhaps it will only be in the months after we've left this country that, in vivid flashes of recollection and conversation, we'll again savour these experiences.

VIEW OF CHRISTCHURCH FROM BRIDLE PATH

We hike to Bridle Path's highest point on the saddle below Mount Cavendish. As we gaze out over Christchurch, a paraglider sails out from behind Castle Rock. His parachute is red against the silver sunlight reflected from buildings in Christchurch and the white mist obscuring the faraway Southern Alps. The glider floats peacefully and touches down on the red landing target in a grassy field.

We also begin our descent, romping down the Heathcote side of Bridle Path before catching the Christchurch Gondola for a six-minute ride up to Mount Cavendish's summit where a sweet treat awaits us in the restaurant at the top. Then, while low winter sun casts stark shadows over the volcano rim – even as it bathes Lyttelton Harbour and Banks Peninsula in golden light – we tramp Crater Rim Walkway to where it intersects with Bridle Path. Vilis photographs one last New Zealand stile, this one's weathered wood almost white against shadows on the hills, the barbed-wire fence's barbs like spiky beads on a necklace.

In gathering dusk, we hurry down Bridle Path to Lyttelton and return to the rink in time to watch the most senior skaters perform. Jānis looks shy and proud when he steps forward to accept his trophy cup during presentations after the competition. "*You* had a good skate today," an older boy tells him. "You're from Canada, aren't you?"

June 6

GROUND MIST cloaks the streets of Lincoln, diffusing the orange light of street lamps, blurring the edges of buildings, and muting the dawn chorus of winter bird song. I collect our milk from the bottle compartment below the mailbox then return to the house, the smell of wood smoke sharp and bitter in the air.

During the morning, the boys finish their few remaining pages of schoolwork and record recent Scouting memories in their

Cub and Scout diaries. Then I open Elsie Locke and Ken Dawson's *The Boy with the Snowgrass Hair*, and we follow the fictional adventures of Tom and Lou – two tramping teens who are part of a foursome exploring Mahitahi River Valley south of Fox Glacier. There, wild rivers threaten to sweep the trampers off their feet, huge boulders – "goolies" – block their passage, and a hut-loving possum tests their mettle and ingenuity. The book whets our appetite for our own adventures in glacier country.

IN LATE afternoon, girl screams mesh with boy yells as Ruchika and Sachin join Dainis and Jānis in a wild game of tag. I see heads flash past the house windows and catch glimpses of bodies vaulting over the fence or erupting from behind a barrier of flax. This house I will always remember, not for itself or anything in it, but for the volatile play of children in its yard.

BEFORE BEDTIME, Dainis and Jānis play *Worms 2* on the laptop. "Now, this is a *real* New Zealand game!" Jānis crows, grinning up at me. "It's got bungy jumping, paragliding, sheep – and best of all, it has *Supersheep!*"

I glance over his shoulder to the laptop screen, on which a miniature white sheep blasts into virtual sky. A red cape flares above its back as it soars upward and across the screen, after which it missiles down to detonate on impact with a squirming pink worm. How appropriate that in New Zealand, my sons would find a superhero that's a sheep!

June 8

THE CANTERBURY landscape lies quiet, its roadsides and pastures accented by winter's blackened browns. Bare trees and sombre evergreens stand beside the highway like mourners at summer's graveside. Today, we make our glacier run through Arthur's Pass.

In Porter's Pass, snow dusts tawny mountains. Farther on, the limestone tors and jumbled grey rocks of Castle Hill Conservation Area appear frozen in time. "They remind me of Stonehenge," Vilis murmurs. "A natural Stonehenge."

CASTLE HILL CONSERVATION AREA

The sun drops low in the northwest as Vilis navigates the wicked curves in Arthur's Pass. At the top of the pass, we drive at snow level, the mountains close and cold around us. The boys list names of roadside features that drip warning and intrigue: Death's Corner, Candy's Bend, Starvation Point. *Who was Candy? Who starved?*

At Kūmara Junction, we link up with the coastal highway and follow it south, pushing hard to reach Hokitika before nightfall. *Rimu* trees drape woodland edges with curtains of weeping twigs. Forests thick with tree ferns speak poems of moisture. Near Hokitika, forest gives way to scrub and flax swamps that are replaced by wind-sculpted thickets intermingled with pastures.

On reaching Hokitika, we book into a motel. The boys are rowdy, filled with pent-up energy after four hours in the car. From the top bunk bed in our room, Jānis sings lines from a poem about New Zealand prospector Arawata Bill, " 'Some people shave in the mountains. But not so–' " He flings his body into the air and dives down onto the cushioning softness of a double bed against the opposite wall of the small room..." 'Arawata Bill who let his whiskers grow!' "[36]

"Yeah!" Dainis shouts, then launches himself from the bunk onto the bed after Jānis vacates it.

"They sure are wild," Vilis says admiringly.

June 9

RAIN MUTES Hokitika this morning, the pillared arches of the town's clock tower leading our gazes upward to four clock faces and the spire-topped cupola above them. Founded during the 1860s' gold rush, Hokitika is now a showcase for jade. Sheltered by umbrellas, we wander downtown streets and visit galleries and gift shops featuring jade carvings and jewellery, the precious stone showing different shades of green. Some carvings are laced with milky white, and some are the deep, rich emerald of the river pools we dunked ourselves in at Bark Bay on Abel Tasman Coast Track.

Velvet roadsides accompany us south along the West Coast toward Ōkārito, the coastal town where two weeks ago snow lay on the ground for the first time in recorded history. At Harihari, ditches are flooded, with water still lapping at the highway's edge. This lush wetness is so different from the rain shadow east of the Southern Alps. The Christchurch area receives only sixty-five centimetres of annual rainfall.[37] In contrast, the West Coast is drenched by fallout from clouds that accumulate moisture while sailing above the

Tasman Sea. When those clouds collide with the Southern Alps, they unload precipitation onto the coast as the moisture rises into cooler air. Punakaiki, in the north – where we hiked to Pancake Rocks and Fox River Cave – receives more than two metres of rain each year. Fiordland, in the far south, is drenched by more than six metres of annual rain. Parts of south Westland, where we're headed, receive a staggering *ten metres* or more of rain every year.[38] *How much of that rain will we experience during the next three days?*

ON ŌKĀRITO COASTAL WALK

In Ōkārito, a torrential downpour blasts the coast and town. Undeterred, we tramp part of the Ōkārito Coastal Walk, with rain cascading in rivulets down our rain coats, pants, and boots. Beside us, the Tasman Sea slams onto a stony beach and piles white froth knee-deep. The boys race through the foamy drifts. Inland, steep-sided hills and forested cliffs tower over us, their rain-soaked shades of green split by waterfalls that pour yellow tannin-laden water over sheer cliff edges.

Abel Tasman made his first sighting of "a large, high-lying land" – previously unknown to Europeans – offshore from these cliffs.[39] And it was here, in a fictitious town, that Booker-prize-winning novelist Keri Hulme's tormented characters Kerewin Holmes and Simon P. and Joe Gillayley in *The Bone People* tangled and shattered and finally entwined their lives.[40] This place is stone and tree, sea and sky, water falling from clouds and cliffs.

After leaving the storm-drenched beach, we drive south to the village of Fox Glacier. It's one of a handful of small, isolated settlements scattered along the narrow coastal plain that cater to tourists visiting Westland Tai Poutini National Park. We book into a two-level motel flat in late afternoon darkness and hang our rain gear and wet clothes on every conceivable knob and protuberance on both flat levels, hoping our gear will be dry by morning. Then a roar like the sudden beating of a thousand drums reels us back to the flat's doorway. We shrink beneath a small overhanging roof and stare in stunned disbelief at the liquid fury the night sky unleashed. Not even in Ōwhango did we experience such violent rain.

What will morning bring?

June 10

DAINIS PULLS his toque lower over his ears. "It's cold!"

Cold, it is – but at least it's dry as we wait on the shore of Lake Matheson, hoping to catch a mirror view of the sunrise over New Zealand's highest mountains. Fringes of *rimu* twigs hang above our heads, and flax leaves look like black swords against the blue sky reflected in the water. Our breaths puff white moisture into clear, frigid air.

Finally, the sun chases away wisps of cloud and reveals the lumpy, jutting head of Mount Tasman and the neat point of Mount

Cook, which the Māori named Aoraki, "The Cloud Piercer." The peaks are reflected on the surface of Lake Matheson, their shapes clearer, their colours brighter on water than in air. Vilis snaps photograph after photograph, bent on capturing the perfect reflected image.

An hour later, we return to our motel flat to pack up. Then we drive Glacier Road to Fox Glacier. Signs along the road alert us to past locations of the glacier's toe, which retreated for much of the last century and is now in an advancing phase:[41] IN 1750 THE GLACIER WAS HERE; IN 1935 THE GLACIER WAS HERE.

At the road's end, we tramp the Fox Glacier Valley Track over a bed of glacial rubble to where the ice river descends from the mountains. Blue and cracked, laden with boulders and gravel, Fox Glacier rests in shadow, the early morning sun lighting the mountaintops above it. Cast-off chunks, blocks, and eroded lumps of ice litter the rubble. Their clear blue intensity pervades the air and tints the shadowed landscape ice blue.

Kea – New Zealand's alpine parrots – skulk among the boulders. A glacier-viewer, less cautious than we are, stands at the foot of the fractured ice face that looms stories high above him.

Using pocket knives, Dainis and Vilis chip slivers and chunks from a stranded ice boulder. Behind them, grey Fox River drains melt water from the glacier. In her poem *A Winter Daybreak*, Anne Glenny Wilson – who lived most of her life on a prosperous New Zealand station – wrote:

> From the dark gorge, where burns the morning star,
> I hear the glacier river rattling on
> And sweeping o'er his ice-ploughed shingle bar.[42]

That's the sound we hear.

"Want to try some?" Vilis passes Jānis and me hand-size

chunks of ice, and we all suck on water frozen into a glacier thousands of years ago, long before humans set foot on this land.

AT FOX GLACIER

In early afternoon, sunshine warms us as we cross Fox River on a swing bridge, intent on tramping 2.5-kilometre Chalet Lookout Track, which is reputed to have a fantastic view of Fox Glacier. From openings in the bush along the track, we catch views of the glacier, its face still shadowed, its upper reaches a white slash between blocky mountainsides scarred by gigantic landslides. Near Chalet Lookout, the track emerges onto a jumbled mass of boulders bordering deep, fast Mills Creek. We scout upstream and downstream for a safe crossing and step experimentally onto rocks, only to retreat. At last we give up, unwilling to chance a winter dunking and bruises in the icy creek fortified by last night's downpour. Tree ferns soothe our disappointment on the return tramp, their flaring crowns vivid green in the coastal rainforest.

After returning to the car, we drive twenty-five kilometres

north from Fox Glacier to Franz Josef Glacier, the second glacier in Westland Tai Poutini National Park that's easily accessible from the coastal highway. The wind is up and bitter as we hike the short but steep Sentinel Rock Walk to the summit of Sentinel Rock, a forested *roche moutonée* or "sheep-back rock" smoothed into a rounded shape by glacier movement in Waiho River Valley. From the summit, we can't see the glacier, only the river's broad gravel bed. Disappointed and chilled by the wind, we don't linger.

In Franz Josef, a small town a few kilometres from the glacier, we rent a cabin in a holiday park and cook pasta and chilli for a hot, hearty supper. Vilis looks up from a local newspaper. "Snow is down to three hundred metres."

Tomorrow, we'll climb Roberts Point Track to a lookout high above Franz Josef Glacier and perhaps encounter some of that snow. This evening, all we seek is warmth.

June 11

AT FIRST light, bold peaks puncture a clear blue sky. Thick frost coats the Blue Bomb with hoary roughness, and icicles hang from an open window in the communal bathroom at the holiday park. In our cabin, we have no hot water.

"The gas cylinders are frozen up," the attendant explains when Vilis and I report the problem.

Vilis shakes his head. "It must not get this cold very often."

Concerned about track conditions, we stop in at the Department of Conservation Visitor Centre in Franz Josef village and request tramping information for Roberts Point Track. The receptionist, a brisk, middle-aged woman, tells us, "I don't know if I'd send anyone up there today. Maybe tomorrow, after things have dried out. You see, you're on bare bedrock, and it can be very slippery." She looks us over. "But if there are a couple of you going, and if you've got a pole, you should be all right."

PETER'S POOL

Like a talisman, Peter's Pool near the start of Roberts Point Track lies perfectly still in mid-morning light. It creates a mirror edged with gilded vegetation against a backdrop of snow-capped peaks. Franz Josef Glacier is a thin smear of white at the base of those peaks, almost hidden by steep, forested mountainsides that we'll traverse to reach Roberts Point, a lookout over the glacier's descending tongue.

The first section of track is a broad gravel path carpeted with leaves. We cross Waiho River on Douglas Bridge, its suspension cables shining like spider webs in the sunlight. On the river's east side, we trek upward across a mountainside, the coastal rainforest dank and dark around us. The track narrows and clings to the steep slope. A railed set of wooden steps leads us over a drop-off. Farther on, we creep around and down a bare rock corner aided by a cable strung between thin iron posts imbedded in rock at the path's edge. Tree ferns cast green kaleidoscopic views against the sky, and we toss a quick look into a corrugated iron hut beside the track. At a sheer rock wall, the path disappears entirely, and we step onto a gallery (suspended boardwalk). Fern fronds flare from niches in the bare rock beside us. The rainforest grows upward below us. We feel like we're walking on air.

Beyond this point, the track becomes a medley of shadowed rainforest paths, mountain-hugging rock trails, and hanging galleries that bypass sheer walls. It seems strange to see the sun as we step out from the forest onto a narrow creek bed. As we climb higher, bush gradually gives way to subalpine shrubland interspersed with outcroppings of bedrock. Ice shines in pockets in the rock and sheets wet surfaces. Jānis slips on a section of icy track we can't avoid, and Vilis's hand darts out to grab him.

"This is a dangerous track!" Jānis blurts in fright. "They should close it!"

"People don't have to go on it," Vilis tells him calmly as we ease our way onto dry bedrock. "We didn't have to come." He pauses, and then adds, "Let's have a rest. We've been pushing hard."

We sit on dry granite in the sunshine and gaze out over the

glacier valley. The coastal rainforests look like velvet, and Waiho River resembles silver ribbons tossed onto grey stone. In my imagination, a cluster of wooded islands in the riverbed is a herd of giant, shaggy elephants grazing on silver pasture.

Rested and soothed by the sun's warmth, we tramp the remaining short distance to Roberts Point through shrubland interspersed with bedrock. From the lookout, we gaze down at the descending tongue of Franz Josef Glacier and at countless waterfalls that cascade in white tendrils down rock faces on the glacier's far side. We spot black specks that are people walking on the glacier's surface and marvel at the wrinkled crevasses that score the ice river. Vilis boils water for hot chocolate, and we picnic at a weathered table. In the distance, the glacier and ice fields draped over mountain peaks provide a glorious backdrop for one of our last outdoor meals in this country.

AT ROBERTS POINT LOOKOUT

The boys, their voices filled with the thrill of exploration, cheerfully tackle the downhill tramp and investigate the hut we passed by so quickly on the way up. Again, we creep around bare rock walls, and again we step onto hanging galleries and stare down at the coastal rainforest beneath us. Five hours after we first passed its peaceful shore, Peter's Pool still lies serene and reflective, welcoming us safely down from the mountain.

We drive north to Hokitika and book into the same room in the same motel we stayed in en route to the glaciers. The boys' eyes are alight with mischief. Within minutes they're diving from top bunk to double bed, their hair tossing wildly.

June 12

THE HIGHWAY verge is white with frost when we depart Hokitika after breakfast. Snow flecks eastern mountaintops with cold cream. Black swans and ducks float in rectangular lagoons near the sea, where waves now roll peacefully onto the shore. A misty coast stretches northward toward Punakaiki and Paparoa National Park, where last month we camped in mist and tramped to beautiful, brooding Cave Creek.

Soon we turn east, heading for Arthur's Pass and Canterbury. We pause to gas up in Kūmara, a tiny village of small, blocky houses with steeply pitched roofs. The houses, painted pastel shades of pink, yellow, and green, possess the same unembellished character as Ōkārito's houses, what little we could see of them in the driving rain. Farther inland near Jacksons, lonely farmhouses in valleys trail smoke from their chimneys. In Ōtira Gorge, the mountains close in on us. When we pull off at a scenic rest stop, a *kea* swoops down to investigate and perches on the station wagon's side mirror. Each of the parrot's bronze-green feathers is edged with dark brown, creating the impression that the bird's lustrous plumage was exactingly carved from iridescent wood. At the top of Arthur's Pass, icicles drip from a road cut next to tussock and heath.

"I like this vegetation up here," Vilis murmurs. "It looks alpine. It looks cold. I like that."

East of the pass, we cross Waimakariri River on a long, single-lane bridge that has pull-offs to allow oncoming traffic to pass. It tingles a few nerves, but doesn't hold a candle to the shared *highway and railway bridge* we crossed during our excursion to Punakaiki last month. At Craigieburn, thin snow crusts the ground, and at Sheffield, Canterbury's hedges lead us home.

"SO, DID you get your Silver Kiwi?" I ask Jānis when he bounces into the house after attending Cubs. Two weeks ago, he presented his twentieth Kiwi Project, his Cub diary.

"Yup. And they gave me this!" His eyes shine as he touches a half-black, half-red scarf fastened around his neck with a braided leather woggle. Ten months after Jānis's first anxious Cub meeting, the Lincoln Koreke Cub Pack has claimed him as one of its own.

June 14

AN UNEXPECTEDLY warm wind teases me when I step outside to call the boys in for tea. This morning, the voices of Coffee Club skaters discussing the nor'wester were filled with the same hope and near-reverence that infuses a Canadian's mention of the word "spring."

"The boys are enjoying it here more and more every day," Vilis comments when I re-enter the house. "Pretty soon they won't want to leave! And it's all because they have friends now."

Suddenly, the house is filled with a half dozen red-cheeked children ranging in age from six to thirteen. They all troop down the hall to Jānis's room. There, Jānis presents Josh with three plastic milk jugs filled with dried peas for slingshot ammunition. He also gives Sam the two, long exquisite peacock feathers he found in the campground at Ōrewa the day we visited Tiritiri Mātangi Island in January.

Then the neighbour kids are gone, supper is eaten, and my men are out the door, walking to the Scout Hall. Once again, the Scouts will shoot target rifles at the range in Tai Tapu.

I embrace the winter evening with a walk beneath Lincoln's street lights. The warm wind that earlier buffeted leaves is no more than a whisper now, gently rustling tenacious oak leaves in Liffey Reserve. Somewhere in the distance, heavy bass music is a muted pulse of sound. The arched windows of St. Stephen's Anglican Church are lit from within, showing warm brown wood through the clear panes. A block away, cigarette smoke, jumbled conversations, and the smell of stale beer drift into the night through an open window of the Famous Grouse Hotel. No one is hooning (driving recklessly) – at least not yet – and Lincoln's main drag, Gerald Street, is as serene as the floodlit face of the library – pale, cool, and a little aloof in its new coat of paint.

"Well, I improved my score over last time," Dainis tells Vilis and me when he returns from Scouts. "By twenty points. I scored seventy-two this time." The first time, we had just moved to Lincoln, and everything was new. This time, Dainis felt right at home.

June 16

THIS MORNING, rain taps a raucous tune on the garage roof. Inside, Vilis paces while I sip a mug of Milo and accept bills and coins from garage-sale hunters who move in, scan our goods, and snatch out what they want before hurrying away to find the next bargain. At noon, we close and lock the garage door. The rest are giveaways.

IN LATE afternoon, Dainis and Jānis cross the street to visit the Peters family while Vilis and I attend supper parties in Christchurch. Mine is a goodbye Coffee Club potluck. His is dinner at the home of Landcare's boss, Oliver Sutherland.

Vilis drops me off at Daphne's house. She greets me with a huge smile. Her home is welcoming, with bookshelves stuffed with books, lots of photos on the walls, and comfortable easy chairs.

A number of Coffee Club regulars are already in attendance, and I gather snatches of conversations that jump from skating to underwater hockey, and from distances between Australian towns to who made the pumpkin pie (which, unlike my disastrous October attempt, tastes delicious). Some skaters have brought a partner or child with them, and young voices and laughter mingle with those of adults.

Daphne's kitchen is a flurry of activity. Her husband fills tall-stemmed glasses with wine or juice, and a skater named Brian agitatedly stirs a rice dish.

"Hi, Brian. How are you?" Jane, who competes in local skating competitions, asks in her gentle voice.

"Rather flustered at the moment," he replies, shifting his weight restlessly.

"Would you like the burner on?" Jane reaches across the range top to turn on the burner. Then she arranges to use the oven to caramelize brown sugar for a cake topping. "It's so nice to see everyone not in their skating clothes," she comments, and I agree.

Coach Chris Street, who's sitting on the kitchen counter, informs the gathering that the record number of skaters on the ice during public skating was 591, two or three years ago. Kim Lewis joins Chris on the counter and answers his cell phone, but the call is for a third coach, and all three burst out laughing.

The food is fantastic: fruit, seafood, exotic and homestyle dishes, lots of desserts. After the meal, Jane presents me with an orchid and a card signed by many Coffee Club skaters. A small pair of white skates dangles from the top of the card. Humbled and reminded of all the intense and enjoyable hours I spent with this eclectic group of skaters, I thank everyone fondly. Then I call a taxi, having made arrangements to meet Vilis at the Sutherland home.

A Blue Star taxi soon arrives, and I leave the party, which is still in full swing. Amid cheerful farewells tossed my way, Jane says earnestly to the group, "We can do this more often. We don't have to wait until somebody leaves."

After the boisterous atmosphere in Daphne's home, the cab's silence is startling.

"Are you having a good evening, ma'am?" the driver asks politely.

"Yes, I am. Is it a busy evening for you?"

"Not yet, but it will be later, starting around one o'clock."

"When the pubs close?" I ask.

"That's just it. They don't close."

City lights shine through haze, softening the streets. I watch the dollars add up on the meter while the driver and I continue our desultory conversation. I tell him that my family is living in New Zealand for a year.

"Taking a break from G. W., are you?" (He means George W. Bush, the American President.)

"Actually, I'm Canadian, not American," I respond.

"Oh. Are you enjoying yourselves here?"

"Very much." It doesn't phase me a bit that he mistakenly

identified me as an American. Here, half a world away from my home, I appreciate that others might not distinguish between an American and a Canadian accent.

I arrive at Oliver and Ulla's house just as they and their Landcare-associated guests – Vilis, John Parkes, and another senior Landcare researcher and his wife – finish a dessert of chocolate mousse and thin coconut cookies. Māori love songs play in the background.

"That's some nice *pounamu*," Oliver comments, studying my jade and gold earrings when I take a seat beside him at the dining table.

"Thank you. Vilis bought them for me."

"He's got good taste."

Conversation focuses on the new humane trap a Landcare researcher had a part in developing, and then becomes an intense discussion of Oliver's retirement plan to rid Durville Island of stoats. On a different tack, John tells a witty, naughty story about a Landcare meeting that has us all chuckling. Throughout the conversation, part of my attention is captivated by the Māori songs, which are rhythmic and soothing.

On the drive home to Lincoln, the Blue Bomb's headlights punch veiled holes through thick fog. Oliver has offered to buy the station wagon for the same amount we paid for it, although Vilis and I told him the left side is now dented due to my claustrophobic inability to park in the garage. Oliver shrugged and said he was looking for an inexpensive car for someone who will use the station wagon much as we have. I shake my head, thinking that his generosity is astounding, even as I hold the CD of Māori love songs he gave me simply because he noticed how much I enjoyed listening to them.

June 17

TODAY, WE'RE welcomers at Lincoln Baptist Church, greeting all who enter. Elizabeth Peters joins us, and we make it a laughter-filled race to see who can hand out the bulletins first. During the service, Elizabeth plops herself onto Dainis's lap. He looks startled and uncomfortable, but doesn't ask her to get down.

After the service, lunch at the Peters' home is a giddy affair, with our two families squeezed around the rectangular dining room table. Tucked-in elbows are crammed against tucked-in elbows. The six children all talk at once, making adult conversation a tenuous venture frequently interrupted. I sit between Ben and Elizabeth and receive continuous requests to dish out oven-fried potato strips and chicken nibbles, too many of which come from Dainis, whom I would nudge with my foot under the table if I could I reach him. While I contemplate ways to deliver this hint, Sam pours tomato sauce over his coleslaw as well as his potatoes and chicken, and threatens to pour it on his pavlova, too. Elizabeth drinks and eats exactly what Dainis drinks and eats, asking for a small piece of pavlova to taste, just as he does. Dainis and Sam begin to cook a slice of celery over a candle. In the midst of all this, dark-haired Christine – mother of the vibrant Peters brood – calmly explains how she made the elderberry juice. Josh proudly adds that he made the pavlova, and that Ben baked the banana bread, which we also eat for dessert with fresh pineapple.

After the meal, the children vacate the table as though sucked from the room by a wild wind. Peace sweeps into the vacuum, and part of me lays down a shield I didn't know I was holding.

"HI! I didn't see you coming. Welcome!" Andrea calls to us.

It's good to be back at her and Andy's home in West Melton.

The beautiful wooden furniture and richly coloured walls feel familiar. Again, as on our first day in New Zealand, we dine on lasagne, and we also enjoy apple crisp baked from Andrea's home-grown Granny Smith apples, as well as chocolate chip ice cream and Vilis's home-made chocolates. This evening, my family isn't battling jet lag exhaustion – like we were that first day ten and a half months ago. From start to finish, today has been a day of sharing, of warm handshakes and smiles, of beginning to let go of this land.

After the meal, we play Jenga. The tower of miniature wood slabs grows higher and higher with each player's turn. On our last attempt, we manage to balance thirty levels of blocks, impossibly decked one on top another. Jānis accidentally bumps the tower with his thumb and sends the blocks crashing down onto the table amid our laughter. Like those falling blocks, our New Zealand experiences will tumble onto the tarmac of Christchurch International Airport six days from now.

June 18

CUBS FREEZE when we enter St. Nicholas Scout Hall in Christchurch. They stare at Jānis and Dainis in their tan, red-sashed Canadian Cub and Scout uniforms – strikingly different from the New Zealand Cubs' dark green uniforms.

One boy looks from us to his leader. "Are we in trouble?"

"Welcome to St. Nicholas Cub Pack," the leader greets us warmly, before introducing us to the Cubs. They now eye us curiously.

Thus begins Dainis's and Jānis's presentation about Canada to the Christchurch Cubs. They quiz the Kiwi Cubs about some basic Canadian geography, show them Canadian stamps, coins, and the Canadian flag Dainis borrowed from the Lincoln Scout Troop. They describe typical Canadian clothes and sports, and Vilis and I help them sing *Land of the Silver Birch*. They pass around maple candy Vilis made and teach their hosts to count to ten in French. Lastly, they divide the host Cubs into three groups and join them in a predator/prey game of wolves, raccoons, and ants.

Forty minutes seem like five. When we leave, the St. Nicholas Pack crowds around us, thanking the boys again and again. One red-haired Cub begs Vilis for the recipe to make maple candy.

June 19

THIS EVENING, Vilis and Jānis return from Cubs with Ruchika and Sachin Tandon in tow, since their parents aren't home. During the Cub meeting, the Lincoln Cubs visited the Halswell Pack, and at Pack Down (ending ceremony), Jānis had the privilege of lowering the New Zealand flag.

Vilis places several thin logs in the small log burner between the kitchen and living room.

"Do you have a fire?" Ruchika asks in surprise.

"Yes." Vilis opens the stove door and shows her the flames. "We need it in winter."

"Is it cold where you live?" she asks.

"Yes," Vilis says. "On a really cold night it can drop to about thirty degrees below zero." (Celsius)

Ruchika's eyes widen and her mouth drops open.

"In other places I've lived," Vilis tells her, "it gets to fifty degrees below zero."

Her eyes and mouth gape even wider.

My husband invites Ruchika and Sachin into the living room, where they and our boys sit among packed suitcases, suck maple candy, and chat about why we're living in New Zealand and do we really have 150 boxes of belongings packed up at our house in Canada. Then we see car lights. The Tandon parents are home. Our young guests bid us smiling goodnights.

IN THE clear cold of night, my family strides to the rugby field one last time to shoot off the remaining fireworks we bought for Guy Fawkes Day more than half a year ago. The stars are brilliant shards of light, the milky way a band of celestial dust smeared across the night by an unseen hand. The fireworks hiss, pop, and squeal as they shoot out white, green, and pink streaks and cascades of light. Vilis and I spin sparklers in big circles while the boys toss their sparklers into the air – they splash white flames against the night. "They're like *poi*," Vilis murmurs. When the sparklers die, we hurry home under the Southern Cross – that aloof swan of the southern night, winging across the sky above us.

June 20

FOR SO long, Mount Bradley has beckoned to me from Banks Peninsula's Crater Rim Walkway and Summit Road. Now it looms over us. Three days before my family will leave this country, we tramp over tawny grassland tufted with *kānuka* trees, our goal: to approach Kaituna Pass from the opposite side of the pass to the section of Mount Bradley Walkway we tramped in late October, and then scale Mount Bradley.

As we climb, the *kānuka* disappears, leaving tussocks of grass standing like unkempt shocks of grain on close-cropped pasture. On the pass's saddle, a rock outcrop provides a picnic table for our final outdoor New Zealand meal. Winter sun paints the landscape with light and shadow and encircles my sons' fair heads with halos of spun gold.

AT KAITUNA PASS

Sign of the Packhorse is solid and welcoming, the hut's views of Lyttelton Harbour and the volcanic crater rim as stunning as they were in October, although the hills are browner now. Dainis and Jānis build a fire in the log burner and lounge near its warmth while we rest before tackling the remainder of our climb. Guarded by steep cliffs on two sides, Mount Bradley's triangular peak is accessible via a long, curving ridge from the hut to the western corner of the triangle. That will be our path.

Outdoors again, we tramp upward over knobby volcanic rock protruding through thin soil, and I envision spitting, frothing lava solidifying into these rounded lumps. Sheep droppings look like plump black seeds scattered everywhere on rocks and cropped grass. When we reach the summit at 855 metres, we gaze out over Canterbury one last time. To the north, rooftops in Lyttelton form a dazzling crescent set against shadowed crater slopes and rich blue harbour. To the east, Kaitorete Spit is a slim wand warding off the massive blue of the Pacific Ocean. Westward, the Canterbury Plain lies blanketed with haze to the foot of the Southern Alps' gleaming, white-topped peaks.

A gusting wind chases us from the summit, but instead of returning to Sign of the Packhorse and following our upward route, we tramp down a steeply descending ridge. In the mountain's shadow, the air is cold, and snow dusts dry grassy tussocks. A flock of sheep grazing far below us is a dim cluster of grey bodies.

JĀNIS AND DAINIS ON THE SLOPE OF MOUNT BRADLEY

The boys, giddy with silliness, concoct a wild story wherein this magnificent, lava-born landscape was created by sheep rather than volcanoes. A moment later, his eyes still dancing, Jānis asks, "What's a sheep's favourite love story?"

"I don't know." I respond. "What?"

"Rameo and Eweliet."

IN LATE afternoon, the voices of our sons and their buddies from across the street grow into excited crescendos while they play tag and capture the flag in our yard. Vilis smiles and turns to me. "Isn't that a lovely sound?"

When it's time for the Peters children to walk home, five-year-old Elizabeth – a golden-haired girl among four boys – slips her hand into Dainis's when she steps out to cross the street.

FRIENDS: SAM, SACHIN, JANIS, RUCHIKA, BEN, DAINIS, JOSH

June 21

DURING MY final skate, the ice dances are like candy held out to a toddler. In my mind, a gown swirls around my ankles while I perform the Dutch Waltz. I hold a rose in my teeth when I step out the Canasta Tango. Convict chains drag at my legs while I labour in the cotton fields of the Baby Blues. Right at the end of the hour, I execute a perfect three turn, the manoeuvre that has eluded me for weeks.

"The light bulb comes on," Chris Street murmurs.

"Did you see that look in her eyes?" Anna, another skater, whispers.

AFTER TEA, Dainis stands straight and slim among the Lincoln Scouts as Dave Lord presents him with a half-red, half-black scarf and a framed photograph of the Lincoln Scout Troop on the porch of the trampers' hut at Lake Daniell. While Dainis lowers the flag, with its Union Jack and Southern Cross, the other Scouts sing *Taps* with unsteady voices.

"See, you, Dainis!" they call as we leave the Scout Hall for the last time. Enveloped by fond memories, we walk home in early winter darkness.

June 22

IN THE Landcare Research lunch room, packets of chips in newsprint, dishes of butter, and piles of white bread cover the table. These are the components of the classic New Zealand treat of chips on buttered bread. The boys and Vilis dig into the tucker, but the sheer volume of starch and cholesterol scare me off. While he eats, Dainis discusses his tracking tunnel project with Wendy Ruscoe, the rat researcher who works in Tongariro Forest. Vilis's soaring, mirth-filled laugh rings out often as colleagues offer him final good wishes. It was his work that brought us to New Zealand, and here it ends.

Vilis's team leader affectionately recaps highlights of my husband's time at Landcare, after which Landcare employees blend their voices in a Māori farewell song. In response, my family sings *Land of the Silver Birch*. This time, we tack on three verses I hastily wrote. The first two verses elicit the laughs I intended. The third becomes a blending of two countries, with Vilis's clear baritone overlaying another Canadian canoeing song onto my sons' and my voices singing of Aotearoa.

DURING THE evening, Nancy and Neal Borrie host us for our final New Zealand tea, offering us good food and a homey atmosphere. We've received gift after gift this week, our souls nourished by acceptance and friendship, our spirits fed by Canterbury's beauty. I've learned a lesson: the heart of this country lies as much in its people as in its riveting landscapes and intriguing birdlife and flora.

June 23

STARS ARE a thousand diamonds in the sky. Christchurch lights spread a sparkling orange-and-white blanket over hills and plain. The roads and streets are empty. Only two startled bunnies hop into grassy verges, and a half dozen cars cruise by while I drive the familiar route to the rink.

Inside, the competitive squad is already on the ice. Kim Lewis arrives, looking as tired as I feel. "Jānis isn't here," I inform her. "He's not well." While we talk about his sore throat and hers, I hand her the trophy cup Jānis earned three weeks ago and accept the progress report she typed madly last evening.

When I drive away, skaters warming up outside the rink appear around corners, like fleet-footed spectres. They race through patches of light, only to disappear into blackness again. I cruise back to Lincoln on auto pilot, the grey paved roads rolling peacefully beneath the Bomb's tires, the clouds above, brushed with faint moonlight.

NIGHT'S SILENCE is pried and chiselled into sound by blackbirds' robin-like calls and starlings' whistles. The sky brightens slowly – a long, brooding dawn on the edge of winter's shortest day. Today, we leave New Zealand.

Before noon, our final packing is done and the yard is filled with children – Nams, Peters, Tandons. Scout leader Dave Lord drops by with Marcus and Braden, and his boys join the crowd for one final romp with Dainis and Jānis.

After lunch, Kim Peters drives my family to the airport, our boxes and suitcases tucked snugly into the trailer we borrowed from him when we moved from North Belt to Maurice Street.

At the airport, we check our baggage. Then we wait while winter casts late afternoon sun onto the Canterbury Plain. Soon dusk falls and our time to board approaches. Then we slip into our seats onboard the Air New Zealand jet. On takeoff, we're tossed into limbo and tumble among time's sand grains, our parachutes bright against the snow of the Southern Alps while we float toward a target on a distant shore.

EPILOGUE

Summer, 2001

Smog blankets the southern Ontario landscape as the Via Rail train carries Vilis, Dainis, Jānis, and me east from Toronto, where we visited Vilis's parents before resuming our homeward journey to northern Nova Scotia. The smog lifts in Quebec, revealing long, narrow farm fields abutting the St. Lawrence River – legacy of the seigneurial system of land ownership instituted by Cardinal Richelieu in seventeenth-century New France.

From Quebec, we travel southeast through New Brunswick, with its dark forests, and then enter Nova Scotia. With every clack of the wheels I feel myself letting go of New Zealand: the Southern Alps, the Canterbury Plain, Banks Peninsula and Crater Rim Walkway, North Island's cluttered rainforests, and the wild cries of kiwi in the night.

Fascinating. When we exited the airport in Toronto after our flights from Christchurch to Auckland, Auckland to Los Angeles, and Los Angeles to Toronto, I was struck by the entirely unexpected realization that Canada's air smells different from New Zealand's. And suddenly so familiar, with its scents of birches and pines and poplars, of grasses and goldenrod and water. I had never before realized that air takes on the essence of a country, but it makes sense that it would, just as vegetation varies widely around the world. That deliciously familiar scent was like a perfume worn by my first love – my homeland.

As we drive the long access road to our property, Ravenhill,

Dainis and Jānis chatter excitedly. Often during our time in New Zealand, they yearned for this place and their friends and LEGO. And now we're here. After living in rented houses in Lincoln, our seventy-eight acres seem vast. And so peaceful, after the airports and train stations.

I scan the yard, noting that grasses, dandelions, and other weeds have invaded my vegetable garden and flowerbeds. I'll have to work hard to restore them, yet that's a small price to pay for ten and a half months of adventure. Apples, cherries, and plums hang from fruit trees, their rounded green shapes camouflaged by wind-nudged leaves. Wild blackberries in the meadows bear green, beaded fruits. While we explored a faraway land, these trees and canes continued their natural cycles without us. At times, my gardener's heart longed for them. Now they're mine once more.

In the house a huge jar filled with massive, mopsy, pink peony flowers – left by our tenant – rests on the kitchen table. He also left various potted perennial bedding plants and a note apologizing for the fact that all my house plants froze one winter day when an improperly closed door blew open.

We haul in our luggage and unpack some of the 150 boxes of belongings stored in the basement. The boys are like fireflies, blinking from one task to the next, with laughter in their voices. Dainis carries the big box of LEGO upstairs, joy radiating from his face. Jānis plays our piano like a hungry child devouring a sandwich. I gaze out each of our home's many large windows, filling my well with views of the nature that surrounds Ravenhill. Vilis checks the house, energized by his leave.

We all pace the deck, calling to the boys' tortoiseshell cats, Blotchy and Baby, cared for by our tenant during our absence. With a graceful leap, Blotchy – ever The Queen – appears on the deck, her elegant steps carrying her straight to Dainis. He scoops her into his arms. Moments later, Baby – slinky, languorous, lovable Baby – winds her way up the steps, purring, her fur incredibly matted. Jānis giggles as she butts her head against his leg. We're home.

AUTHOR'S ENDNOTE

AFTER MY family boarded that Air New Zealand jet on June 23, 2001, we didn't disappear into thin air. We returned to Nova Scotia, Canada, where Dainis and Jānis cuddled their cats, built huge LEGO constructions, played baseball, camped with Cubs and Scouts, and happily renewed friendships. I reclaimed my weedy gardens, harvested fruit to my heart's content, and began to think about transforming my "NZ stories" into a book. Refreshed from being surrounded by ecologists, Vilis resumed his role as professor at the Nova Scotia Agricultural College, now Dalhousie University Agricultural Campus. And, on our very first full day at home, we ate Cheerios for breakfast, Kraft Dinner for lunch, hotdogs for supper, and donuts for dessert – just as Jānis had suggested during one of our hikes in Tongariro National Park.

I like to think that my family's time in New Zealand continued to shape us even after we returned home. We were fit and keen for adventure. Jānis continued figure skating and went on to represent Nova Scotia at two national championships. Dainis returned to winter hockey and played tennis passionately during the summers. Both earned the Chief Scout Award and, after being homeschooled through Grade 9, enrolled in high school and graduated at the head of their classes. Now young men, they're having great fun working as mechanical engineers.

A decade after our New Zealand adventure, Vilis and I enjoyed a year-long leave in Australia – his research focused on dingo movement patterns. We bushwalked through rainforests and deserts, and I bought field guides galore and identified everything I could. We found platypuses, poisonous snakes, and each other again, after spending twenty-one years with our children. I scribbled Aussie observations in small notebooks and blogged about our adventures (visit **www.maginams.ca**). Since our return to Canada, I've begun transforming those observations and posts into a book – *Red Continent: A Year in Australia.*

The world is full of beauty, challenge, and adventure. May it always be so.

GLOSSARY

Aotearoa – Māori name for New Zealand; means "Land of the Long White Cloud" or "Land of the Long Daylight"

haka – war dance, with chanting

hongi – greeting that involves pressing noses

kānuka – shrub or small tree with stringy bark and small, flat leaves

kauri – tall conifer tree with thick, cylindrical trunk and spherical seed cone; among the world's largest trees

kea – alpine parrot

kia ora – hello or thank you

kiekie – climbing vine with tufts of long, narrow leaves

kōtuku – white heron sacred to the Māori

kōwhai – tree with small, paired leaves and yellow flowers; New Zealand's national tree

kunekune – small South Pacific pig

kūmara – yellow-fleshed sweet potato

mānuka – shrub with small, flat, prickly-tipped leaves and white flowers

marae – meeting place; central area of a village

mataī – tall conifer tree; recently peeled bark creates rounded red scars on trunk

moa – extinct flightless bird

nīkau – native palm tree

pāua – abalone

pikirangi – mistletoe

podocarp – coniferous tree that produces a fleshy, berrylike seed cone *poi* – ball; also, a tuft of white feathers dangling from the throat of *tūī*

pounamu, also **greenstone** – New Zealand jade; nephrite

pūkeko – marsh bird with blue-black plumage; swamp hen

rimu – tall conifer tree with weeping twigs

tōtara – conifer tree with stringy bark, flat needles, and fleshy red seed cones

tūī – blackish-brown songbird with two white feather tufts dangling from throat

waka – canoe

weka – woodhen

wharenui – communal house; the focal point of a *marae*

REFERENCES AND NOTES

[1] Keith Sinclair. (2000). *A History of New Zealand.* Auckland: Penguin Books. pp. 14, 19, 29-31.

[2] Ministry for Primary Industries *Manatū Ahu Matua.* (Accessed 6-Mar-2015). "Travel and Recreation: Items to Declare." http://www.mpi.govt.nz/travel-and-recreation/arriving-in-new-zealand/items-to-declare/.

[3] Department of Conservation *Te Papa Atawhai.* (Accessed 6-Mar-2015). "Animal Pests – Stoats." http://www.doc.govt.nz/conservation/threats-and-impacts/animal-pests/animal-pests-a-z/stoats/.

[4] Department of Conservation *Te Papa Atawhai.* (Accessed 6-Mar-2015). "Birds – Kiwi." http://www.doc.govt.nz/conservation/native-animals/birds/birds-a-z/kiwi/.

[5] Thomas D. Isern. (2002). "Companions, Stowaways, Imperialists, Invaders: Pests and Weeds in New Zealand." In *Environmental Histories of New Zealand,* edited by Eric Pawson and Tom Brooking. South Melbourne: Oxford University Press. pp. 241-243.

[6] John Wilson. (Accessed 7-Mar-2015). "Canterbury places – Ellesmere district." *Te Ara* – the Encyclopedia of New Zealand. http://www.teara.govt.nz/en/canterbury-places/page-16.

[7] Isern, pp. 235- 237.

[8] Department of Conservation *Te Papa Atawhai.* (Accessed 6-Mar-2015). "Bats/pekapeka." http://www.doc.govt.nz/conservation/native-animals/bats/.

[9] Margaret Copland. "Welcome to Christchurch." Te Puna Ora Storytelling, Canterbury, New Zealand. Information leaflet.

[10] C. F. Morales, M. G. Hill, and A. K. Walker. (1988). "Life history of the sooty beech scale (*Ultracoelostoma assimile*) (Maskell), (Hemiptera: Margarodidae) in New Zealand *Nothofagus* forests." *New Zealand Entomologist,* 11:24-35; P. D. Gaze and M. N. Clout. (1983). "Honeydew and its importance to birds in beech forests of South Island, New Zealand." *New Zealand Journal of Ecology* 6:33-37.

[11] Gaze and Clout, pp. 33-37.

[12] Laura Sessions. Department of Plant and Microbial Science, University of Canterbury, Christchurch. Interpretive display. (Quoted by kind

permission.)

[13] Elsie Locke. (1973). *The Runaway Settlers*. Victoria, Australia: Penguin Books. pp. 9-22.

[14] Department of Conservation *Te Papa Atawhai*. "Abel Tasman Coast Track, Abel Tasman National Park." Nelson: Nelson/Marlborough Conservancy. (Quoted by kind permission.)

[15] Eric Pawson and Tom Brooking. (2002). "Introduction." *In Environmental Histories of New Zealand*. South Melbourne, Australia: Oxford University Press. p. 6.

[16] Department of Conservation *Te Papa Atawhai*. (1998). "Abel Tasman Parkmap." Historical note reads: "…and once Europeans began to settle this coastline from 1855 they swiftly set about logging the forests and firing the hillsides." Ecological note pertaining to gully forests reads: "Little of this forest has survived in its natural state, but the gullies it once occupied now lead the process of regeneration."

[17] Maggy Wassilieff. (Accessed 12-May-2015). "Shellfish – Sea snails." *Te Ara* – the Encyclopedia of New Zealand. http://www.TeAra.govt.nz/en/photograph/8014/cats-eye-in-shell.

[18] Department of Conservation *Te Papa Atawhai*. (1998) "Abel Tasman Parkmap." Historical notes read: "…Maori occupied sites all along the Abel Tasman coastline… As Awaroa has the largest estuary it was probably the site of the largest and most permanent settlement." Historical note for Awaroa reads: "Awaroa – relics remain as evidence of European settlement; the skeletal remains of the 'Venture' (built here around 1900), school site remains, the derelict homestead of the old farm and a rusting steam engine (once used for crushing beech bark for tanning)."

[19] Leonard Cockayne. (1900). "A Glimpse into the Alps of Canterbury." In *Canterbury Old and New 1850-1900: A Souvenir of the Jubilee*. Christchurch: Whitcombe and Tombs. p. 215.

[20] Wikipedia. (Accessed 12-May-2015). "Botany Bay." http://en.wikipedia.org/wiki/Botany_Bay; information taken from J. C. Beaglehole, editor. (1968). *The Journals of Captain James Cook on His Voyages of Discovery, vol. I: The Voyage of the Endeavour 1768–1771*. Cambridge University Press. p. ccix.

[21] Jean Bartels. (2002). "Introduced Species Summary Project – European Red Fox (*Vulpes vulpes*)." Invasion Biology Introduced Species Summary Project – Center for Environmental Research and Conservation, Columbia University. http://www.columbia.edu/itc/cerc/danoff-burg/invasion_bio/inv_spp_summ/Vulpes_vulpes.htm.

[22] Australian Government, Department of the Environment. (Accessed 12-May-

2015). "Feral Animals in Australia."
http://www.environment.gov.au/biodiversity/invasive-species/feral-animals-australia.

23 Penguin Books. (2000.) *Explore New South Wales*. Victoria: Penguin Books Australia Ltd. p. 63.

24 NSW National Parks and Wildlife Service. (1999). "Visitor Guide, Guy Fawkes River National Park." NPWS Dorrigo District Office, Dorrigo.

25 NSW National Parks and Wildlife Service. (1999). "Visitor Guide, Dorrigo National Park World Heritage Area." NPWS Dorrigo District Office, Dorrigo.

26 E. C. Pielou. (1979). *Biogeography*. Toronto: John Wiley & Sons. pp. 12-14.

27 NSW National Parks and Wildlife Service. (1999). "Visitor Guide, New England National Park World Heritage Area." NPWS Dorrigo District Office, Dorrigo.

28 Christchurch City Council, Parks & Waterways. (Accessed 13-May-2015). "Fact Sheet – Bottle Lake Forest Park."
http://resources.ccc.govt.nz/files/cityleisure/parkswalkways/popularparks/FactsheetBOTTLELAKE-docs.pdf.

29 *Ibid*; Christchurch City Libraries *Ngā Kete Wānanga-o-Ōtautahi*. (Accessed 13-May-2015). "Bottle Lake and Waitikiri: the early years."
http://my.christchurchcitylibraries.com/bottle-lake-waitikiri/.

30 IPENZ Engineers New Zealand. (Accessed 13-May-2015). "Otira Tunnel, Midland Railway." Engineering Heritage New Zealand.
http://www.ipenz.org.nz/heritage/itemdetail.cfm?itemid=63.

31 Department of Conservation *Te Papa Atawhai*. (1999). "Paparoa National Park, Walks in the Punakaiki and Paparoa Area." Hokitika. (Quoted by kind permission.)

32 Department of Conservation *Te Papa Atawhai*. (Accessed 13-May-2015). "Paparoa National Park Resource Summary." (1990).
http://www.doc.govt.nz/Documents/about-doc/role/policies-and-plans/paparoa-national-park-management-plan/paparoa-resource-summary.pdf; pp.7-8.

33 Christchurch City Libraries *Ngā Kete Wānanga-o-Ōtautahi*. (Accessed 13-May-2015). "Cave Creek." http://my.christchurchcitylibraries.com/cave-creek/

34 Department of Conservation *Te Papa Atawhai*. (Accessed 13-May-2015). "Westland petrel/tāiko." http://www.doc.govt.nz/nature/native-animals/birds/birds-a-z/westland-petrel-taiko/; Harper, Mudd, and Whitfield, p. 639.

[35] Mark Pickering. (1999). "Bridle Path and Mount Cavendish." *The Port Hills*. Christchurch: Mark Pickering. pp. 28-29.

[36] Locke and Dawson, p. 101.

[37] Christchurch City Council. (Accessed 13-May-2015). "About Christchurch." Christchurch: The Garden City, New Zealand. http://www.christchurch.org.nz/about/factsstats.aspx.

[33] Andy Dennis. (Accessed 13-May-2015). "Mountains – South Island mountains." *Te Ara* – the Encyclopedia of New Zealand. http://www.TeAra.govt.nz/en/mountains/page-1; Brett Mullan, Andrew Tait and Craig Thompson. (Accessed 13-May-2015) "Climate – Regional climates." *Te Ara* – the Encyclopedia of New Zealand. http://www.TeAra.govt.nz/en/climate/page-2; Climate-Data.Org. (Accessed 13-May-2015). "Climate: Punakaiki." http://en.climate-data.org/location/143240/.

[39] Quoted by Keith Sinclair. (2000). *A History of New Zealand*. Auckland: Penguin Books, p. 30.

[40] Keri Hulme. (1983). *The Bone People*. Baton Rouge: Louisiana State University Press.

[41] Harper, Mudd, and Whitfield, p.652.

[42] Anne Glenny Wilson. *A Winter Daybreak*. In *The New Place: The Poetry of Settlement in New Zealand*. (1993.) Harvey McQueen, editor. Wellington: Victoria University Press. p. 73.

INDEX

Made in the USA
Charleston, SC
07 June 2015